Lost in Wonder, Love, and Praise

Lost in Wonder, Love, and Praise

Prayers for Christian Worship

John R. Killinger

Abingdon Press
Nashville

LOST IN WONDER, LOVE, AND PRAISE
PRAYERS FOR CHRISTIAN WORSHIP

Library of Congress Cataloging in Publication Data

Killinger, John.
  Lost in wonder, love, and praise : prayers and affirmations for Christian worship / John Killinger.
    p. cm.
  Includes index.
  ISBN 0-687-04600-9
  1. Prayers. 2. Public worship I. Title.

BV245 .K542 2001
264'.13—dc21

                                                                2001046167

01 02 03 04 05 06 07 08 09 10 — 10 9 8 7 6 5 4 3 2 1

MANUFACTURED IN THE UNITED STATES OF AMERICA

With love and admiration
for
DAN AND AMELIA MUSSER,
our good friends
on Mackinac Island,
who have meant so much
to so many
and mean even more
to us.

Contents

Introduction

Little can be said about prayer that has not been said before. It is a meeting of God and the people of God's great community, living and dead, and therefore there is nothing else like it in the world. It must be felt, practiced, and experienced to be appreciated.

Perhaps we betray it even by framing it in words, for it is much more than language. It is presence, joy, breath, abandonment, ecstasy. It is losing ourselves in God, being overwhelmed by the Divine Mystery, as if we stood on the shore of a great ocean and felt its mighty waves go over us.

Yet the average person attending religious services has probably never truly known the reality of prayer as presence and abandonment. For this person, prayer is a strange, untouched land of the soul, foreign to everyday experience.

The leader of worship, therefore, has a set task. It is to usher this deprived congregant as close as possible to the vortex of genuine prayer, where he or she may be drawn in and overcome by the sense of God's being. Words must be used—and silence as well—to bait, cajole, and tease the mind into intercourse with the Divine Spirit.

The liturgist is like the matador in a bullfight, and spoken prayers are the red cape. The liturgist turns, feints, pirouettes, flashing the cape this way and that, sculpting the moment with words, pauses, rhythms, until the congregant has been completely drawn into the play and is no longer aware of reluctance or surroundings, but has surrendered to the true spirit of prayer.

Prayers for worship, in other words, are not objects in themselves, any more than the matador's cape is an object in itself. They are the means to an end: to the worshiper's coming into the actual presence of God.

It is always impossible, of course, to predict which prayers will succeed in this high endeavor. There are variant factors each time we worship. Is the sanctuary too warm or too cold? Has the music been uplifting or only indifferent? Are the worshipers tired, bored, excited? Are trucks roaring by on the expressway outside? Is a bird chirping in a nearby bush? Has there been a recent tragedy in the community that draws people together in fear or mourning? Is there a lot of illness and coughing in the congregation? Is the liturgist's voice clear and compelling or weak and depressing?

But we are under fee, as George Buttrick used to say, to produce the very best prayers of which we are capable, to make words bend to the will and mood of communion with God, so that they will mold the very best passes possible, and turn people toward the Divine Presence. T. S. Eliot was right, that words "slip, slide, perish, decay with imprecision";* but they are the best we have, the *only* thing we have, combined with silence, to fashion the cape, to make worshipers charge and turn and stumble into God.

The prayers and affirmations in this book are merely one pastor's attempt to make prayer a greater reality for his congregation. Those that form their nucleus were composed when I was minister of the First Presbyterian Church in Lynchburg, Virginia, a staid but hearty congregation of folk in an old community near the Blue Ridge Mountains. Since then, I have pastored the First Congregational Church of Los Angeles, California, the oldest English-speaking congregation in that metropolis, whose august Gothic sanctuary covers a city block, and the Little Stone Church of Mackinac Island, Michigan, where the congregation each Sunday includes scores of visitors from all over

---

*T. S. Eliot, "Burnt Norton" in "Four Quartets." In *The Complete Poems and Plays* (New York: Harcourt Brace & Co., 1952), p. 121.

the world, but rarely numbers more than a hundred and fifty souls; and prayers composed for these churches have been added to the original number.

The collection is offered with fear and trembling, for the materials that seemed to work in one setting, with one particular congregation, may well fare dismally in another. But they are offered in the hope that they may be adapted to other settings, and that certain ideas or phrasings among them may lead other pastors and liturgists to the composition of new materials for public worship.

And they are offered with this prayer: *That the Holy Spirit, who is the Supreme Matador, will make the final pass and turn us all in toward God, where we shall blissfully die to ourselves and be raised in an incredible newness of life!*

ONE

Calls to Worship

1

Leader: God watched over us as we slept last night.
People: **God was there when we awakened this morning.**
Leader: God is in this place, among us now.
People: **God is in the singing, the silence, the sermon, and the prayers.**
Leader: Let us worship God!

2

Leader: God is the God of all the ages. Let us praise the name divine.
People: **From everlasting to everlasting, God is our God.**
Leader: As the heavens are higher than the earth, so are God's ways higher than our ways.
People: **Let us worship and bow down. Let us sing praises to God's name!**

3

Church bells call us from the world of beauty and adventure around us to the world of beauty and adventure within. "I have heard your voice," says the poet, "and it speaks to me of country lanes and covered bridges, of vast deserts and lush jungles, of great cities and teeming peoples. But it also speaks of angels and demons, of past sins and new possibilities, of tangled lives and blessed redemption." O come, let us worship the God of our salvation, the One who reigns forever in the kingdom of the heart.

4

Leader: The Lord is my strength and my shield;
People: **My heart trusted in God, and I am helped.**
Leader: Therefore my heart greatly rejoices.
People: **And with my song I will praise the Lord.**

5

Leader: O give thanks to God, and call on God's name.
People: **Make known God's deeds among the people!**
Leader: Sing to God, sing praises to God Almighty, tell of God's wonderful works.
People: **Glory in the divine name; let the hearts of those who seek life rejoice!**

6

Leader: God is our rock, our fortress, and our deliverer.
People: **Our God, our rock, in whom we take refuge.**
Leader: God is our shield, and the giver of salvation.
People: **Let us call upon the Lord, who is worthy to be praised!**

7

Something usually happens before a worship service, as if a clan or tribe were gathering and preparing for a serious ritual. There is a gradual intensification of atmosphere, and a kind of expectancy that grows and grows. As the moment is presently reached when the worship begins, it is like a lunge into a new dimension of being, into a sacred experience that will forever change the character and destiny of those gathered. That is why we are here, to be changed by a sacred experience. In the church that is a lengthened shadow of the life and ministry of Jesus, it is he who is most responsible for our patterns of religious understanding. Therefore let us worship God by singing about Jesus.

8

Who shall ascend to the holy hill and worship the Lord of Lords? The person who has clean hands and a pure heart, and whose life is not stained by sin. And who is such a person? Ironically, the very one who feels unclean and impure before God, who cries out, O woe is me, for I am a person of unclean lips, and am not worthy to come into the presence of God!

9

Leader: Most rulers are born in palaces;
People: **Jesus was born in a stable.**
Leader: Most rulers never work for a living;
People: **Jesus was raised in a carpenter's shop.**
Leader: Most rulers ride in fine carriages;
People: **Jesus walked wherever he went.**
Leader: Most rulers die in bed;
People: **Jesus died on a cross.**
Leader: Most rulers reign from a throne;
People: **Jesus reigns from people's hearts.**
Leader: Most rulers rule for a lifetime;
People: **Jesus rules forever!**

10

It is a beautiful day and it is easy to see the spirit of God in the flowers and trees and the land and the sky around us. But we have come into God's house to think about other things: about sin and forgiveness, about love and acceptance, about death and eternal life. And because we are here, the whole world outside should look even more enchanting when we return to it. Therefore let us rejoice in one another's presence, and in the presence of the Holy Spirit. Let us worship God!

11

Leader:	Lord, we believe in you.
People:	**Help thou our unbelief!**
Leader:	Lord, we love you.
People:	**Help us to love you with all our hearts!**
Leader:	Lord, we sing praises to your name.
People:	**Help us to worship you in spirit and in truth!**

12

Leader:	Come, let us give thanks to the Lord!
People:	**Let us bow down before our Maker!**
Leader:	Let us tell of God's love and greatness!
People:	**Let us sing of all that God has done!**

13

This is a very special place, hallowed by the worship of saints for many years. Thousands of souls have stood to sing and knelt to pray in this room. Thousands have heard the word of God here, and have responded by surrendering their hearts to the Divine Spirit. Place has always been important in the worship of God. Therefore it is especially easy to worship God here, where we are surrounded by so many rich and encouraging vibrations. Let us give thanks for this place, and worship God with all our hearts!

14

Leader:	The Lord our God is a mighty God!
People:	**God demands truth and holiness in the world.**
Leader:	The Lord our God is a jealous God!
People:	**Let us turn from our sinful ways and praise God's name.**
Leader:	The Lord our God is a loving God!
People:	**In love let us tune our hearts to worship!**

15

Leader: This is the day God has made.
People: **Let us rejoice and be glad in it!**
Leader: These are the hearts and voices God has given us.
People: **Let us sing and praise and be joyful together!**

16

Leader: The church gathers in the name of Jesus Christ.
People: **We come because we have been called to follow him.**
Leader: We come to worship God in his name.
People: **We come to sing praises and bow down before him.**
Leader: Let us worship in spirit and in truth.

17

There are ghosts here! We sit or stand or kneel with thousands of saints who have worshiped here, and whose lingering presence we can detect if we are sensitive to it. Solomon once said that there is no house sufficient to contain the entire mystery and majesty of God, and that is true. But God's mystery and majesty are easily felt where so many souls have worshiped through the years. Therefore let us be aware, and let us worship God!

18

Leader: Today is a day for remembering.
People: **It is a day for remembering the Creator of the world.**
Leader: It is a day for remembering those who have gone before us in the faith.
People: **It is a day for remembering the death and resurrection of Christ, and the Spirit that came upon his disciples at Pentecost.**
Leader: Let us worship and bow down, let us lift our voices in praise!

19

We live in a place of remarkable beauty, with lovely woods, flowery meadows, rolling hills, and delightful homes. But when the church bells ring, they call us from one kind of beauty to another, and from the God who created the earth to the God who came among us in Jesus Christ and showed us the meaning of everything. Therefore, let us worship the God of all creation and the God of our Lord Jesus.

20

Leader: God is our hiding place.
People: **God will keep us in times of trouble.**
Leader: Let us be glad in the Lord, and rejoice.
People: **Let us shout for joy and praise God's name in song!**

21

Leader: Christ did not come into the world to be served but to serve.
People: **He is in our midst this morning as one who serves.**
Leader: We celebrate our Servant Lord by worshiping God.
People: **Let us sing and pray until we too have become servants!**

22

Leader: We are here today for many reasons.
People: **Some of us are tired, and need a place to rest.**
Leader: Some are lonely, and seek relationship.
People: **Some are afraid, and look for courage.**
Leader: Who is able to meet needs such as ours?
People: **It is God who meets our needs, and we are here because this is where God's presence is celebrated.**
Leader: Then let us worship God.

23

Leader: Welcome to this place of worship.

People: **We come in the name of Jesus Christ.**

Leader: We worship the God who bids us honor our fathers and mothers.

People: **Let us worship God in the name of Jesus and in honor of our fathers and mothers.**

24

Leader: We shall praise you, O God, with all our hearts!

People: **Gladly will we sing and pray to you!**

Leader: We shall bow down in your holy sanctuary.

People: **For your love and faithfulness we will praise your name!**

25

A Call to Worship for Advent

Leader: Let us make a place for God in the wilderness of our hearts.

People: **Let us make a way for God in the desert of our emotions.**

Leader: Let us make room for God in the crowdedness of the season.

People: **Let us worship God now with praise and singing!**

26

A Call to Worship for Christmas

Leader: It is the time of the star and the shepherds.

People: **It is the season of the Savior's birth.**

Leader: Let us surround him now with prayer and caroling.

People: **Let us praise his blessed name!**

27
A Call to Worship for Christmas Eve

Leader: This is the night we have waited for.
People: **It is the most beautiful night of the year.**
Leader: It is the night of shepherds and stables, and of humble people everywhere.
People: **It is the night of our dear Savior's birth!**

28
A Call to Worship for the Sunday After Christmas

Leader: It is over now: the shopping and wrapping, the baking and celebrating.
People: **The Christmas rush is behind us.**
Leader: But the meaning of Christmas lives on and on.
People: **The Lord of Christmas is here among us!**
Leader: Let us worship the Lord of Christmas!

29
A Call to Worship for Palm Sunday

Leader: This is Palm Sunday, when we remember the Triumphal Entry.
People: **Jesus entered the city as people shouted "Hosanna!"**
Leader: But afterward they denied him and demanded his death.
People: **Let him enter our hearts and never be denied.**
Leader: Jesus is the Christ, the anointed one of God.
People: **Jesus is our living Lord!**

30
A Call to Worship for Maunday Thursday

Leader: We are here to remember the Last Supper of our Lord.

People: **We must recall his pain and relive our grief.**

Leader: It is the only way to discover God's forgiveness.

People: **It is the only way to the joy of the Resurrection!**

31
A Call to Worship for Easter

Leader: Christ is risen!

People: **He is risen indeed!**

Leader: Glory and honor, dominion and power be to God for ever and ever.

People: **Christ is risen! Alleluia!**

32
A Call to Worship for Easter

Leader: All the ends of the earth shall remember and turn to the Lord;

People: **All the families of the nations shall worship before him;**

Leader: For dominion belongs to the Lord,

People: **And he rules over the nations.**

Leader: Let us worship God.

33

The hour, the music, the chimes, all call us away from our ordinary world into one that is extraordinary, filled with Spirit and Love and Presence, and bids us kneel to worship in the sure and certain knowledge that God is here. Let us worship God!

34

Leader:	Great is our God, says the psalmist,
People:	**And greatly to be praised!**
Leader:	For God has stretched the heavens above us
People:	**And filled the earth with every good thing.**
Leader:	We live and move and have our being in God,
People:	**And in him is our everlasting hope!**
Leader:	Let us worship God.

35

Leader:	We live in a world filled with wonder:
People:	**The leafing trees and budding flowers,**
Leader:	The restless wind, the flight of birds,
People:	**The rising of the sun and the phases of the moon,**
Leader:	The miracle of our bodies and their motions,
People:	**The gift of our minds.**
Leader:	These alone should call us back to the central mystery of our existence.
People:	**They should return us to God.**
Leader:	Then let us lift our voices in praise and thanksgiving!

36

Leader:	God is our hiding place, says the psalmist.
People:	**A place of refuge, of retreat from the storms of life.**
Leader:	From all the things that are bothering us.
People:	**We are all hiding from something.**
Leader:	Or looking for something that remains hidden to us.
People:	**Perhaps this is the day we'll find it.**
Leader:	Let us worship God and see.

37

Be merciful to me, O God, says the psalmist; be merciful to me, for in you my soul takes refuge; in the shadow of your wings I will take refuge, until the destroying storms pass by. I don't know what storms may be passing by in your life, but you have come to the right place at the right time, and you are very welcome here. Let us worship God!

38

"Clap your hands, all you peoples," said the psalmist. "Shout to God with loud songs of joy. For the LORD, the Most High, is awesome, a great ruler over all the earth." Isn't it true? And aren't we ready to sing? Then let us worship God!

39

The crocuses and the daffodils are blooming. The perfume of spring is in the air. We can feel the presence of God all around us. It is real, it is palpable, it is almost tangible. It cannot be far from such a feeling as this to the spirit of worship. Let us worship God!

40

"O give thanks to the Lord," says the psalmist, "for he is good, and his steadfast love endures forever. Who can utter the mighty doings of the Lord, or declare all his praise?" We can't declare it all—we can't even begin to do that—but we can certainly join the chorus. Let us worship God!

TWO

Opening Prayers

1

We greet you in the morning, O God, as those enfolded in your arms through the night. We praise you for your tender mercies and loving-kindness, and for your faithfulness at times when we have been unfaithful. Now we gather to worship and glorify you in the name of your son Jesus, who taught us to pray, saying, *Our Father. . . .*

✓ 2

We tarry awhile in your presence, O God, in order to be reminded of who we are and what we are made for. Our lives become small and worthless when left to themselves, but open like flowers in the light of your countenance. Help us for the space of this hour to put away all cares and anxieties, all selfishness and ambition, all concern for appearance and popularity, and relax in a spirit of openness and glad reception. Speak to our hearts of the things they need to hear, and heal us of all our sickness and brokenness, that we may lift to you voices of praise and thanksgiving, through Jesus Christ our Lord. Amen.

3

O God, who resides in eternal wisdom and compassion, we turn aside now from other pleasures and pursuits to acknowledge your rulership in our hearts and lives. Help us to lay all our cares and considerations at your feet, and, trusting in your divine love and tenderness, tarry for a while in your healing presence. Make us aware now of our breathing . . . of our hands and bodies . . . of our neighbors in the pews . . . of the sounds in the world around us . . . and of your Spirit in this place. Enable us to pray with the fullness of our own spirits the prayer Jesus taught us to pray, saying, *Our Father. . . .*

4

Your mighty power is always with us, O God, and yet we live as if we were alone. Let this be the hour in which we remember your presence. Change us from a crowd of separate and lonely individuals who experience their own ways into a united people who are seeking your way. And let your love and forgiveness overcome all our doubts, anxieties, and sin, through your son Jesus Christ. Amen.

5

O God of sunrise and sunset, let this be an hour of sunrise in our hearts, when all things are made bright and new. Drive away the shadows of discouragement and loneliness. Raise us up from beds of weariness and despair. Outfit us with joy and excitement for a new day, when we shall walk in the way of Christ Jesus our Lord. Amen.

6

O God, whose presence is known and celebrated in all the earth by singing and praying and clapping and dancing, we bow before you in a moment of confession to thank you for our morality and our complete dependence on you. There is nothing in this life, O God, that we can trust as we trust you. Therefore we praise you for your loving faithfulness, and for the sense of joy and completeness we feel when we are restored to your fellowship. Receive us now, with whatever we have made of our lives, and help us to feel relaxed and renewed in this service, and to be recommitted to you, through Jesus Christ our Lord, who taught us to pray, saying, *Our Father. . . .*

7

O God of hill and valley, of sunshine and thunderstorm, of the tall pines of the forest and the humble forget-me-nots that bloom on the forest floor, we greet you and worship you this day as the maker of all that is, and as the lover and caretaker of our souls. Forgive us for any single hour in which we have not thought of you or inclined our hearts to you, and help us in this hour to find our way back to who we really are in you, and to the joy of your salvation, through Jesus Christ our Lord, who taught us to pray, saying, *Our Father. . . .*

8

O God, who has made of all the peoples of the earth one people, and of all congregations of worshipers one congregation, we praise you this morning for the great legacy of song and worship we enjoy as members of the Christian community. We confess that we have often lived in isolation from other strands of our community, and in so doing have injured the memory of our Lord Jesus, who prayed that we might all be one in him. Mend our brokenness, dear God, and lift our vagrant spirits by your amiable, redeeming presence, that we may experience together the joy of Christ, who taught us to pray, saying, *Our Father. . . .*

9

We love your kingdom, O God, with its promise of justice, its feeling of compassion, its dimensions of joy and hope, its sense of eternity. In our times of darkest despair, it encourages us. In our moments of deepest exhaustion with life and the human enterprise, it bids us stand and go forward. Therefore we pray for those this morning who have come here tired and discouraged for any reason, that they may remember that your kingdom is both now and forever, and that the seeds of belief and trust may be reawakened in their lives, to bring them once more to a harvest of love and excitement in living. Help us to voice to you our most intimate thoughts, and, having done so, to find healing and support for our entire existence. Through Jesus Christ our Lord, who taught us to pray, saying, *Our Father. . . .*

10

O God of sights and sounds and truth and feelings, we praise you for the softness of children's flesh, the feel of the grass under bare feet, the sweet smell of summer rain on hot pavement, the abundance of flowers in the earth, the sense of worship in a place like this. Receive us now, rich in things but poor in soul. Set us on your knee like little children. Hear the humble prayers we make and the songs we sing, and renew us for life in your beautiful world. Through Jesus Christ our Lord. Amen.

11

O God, who has ringed us about with evidence of your loving care, from the sunlight we saw at the dawn of the day and the first breath we drew with consciousness to the food we tasted at breakfast and the beauty of the world through which we passed to come here, we praise you with song and prayer and spoken word, knowing that before anything came into being, you were, and after everything has had its day and is no more, you will be. Teach us to number our days and know their value, and especially to apply ourselves to those spiritual truths and values that will prepare us for eternal life in your kingdom. Let love and peace and joy flow down like a great river, and baptize us in the glorious fire of your presence, through Jesus Christ our Lord. Amen.

12

O God of the seasons, of springing grass and falling leaves,
O God of the world, of sprawling oceans and towering
mountains,
O God of our lives, of birth and death and all the moments
between,
We praise you this morning for the gift of awareness:
awareness of place and people and flowers and music;
awareness of our bodies, our feelings, our failures, our
futures.
Tune our voices to exalt you and our spirits to commune
with yours,
that we may rightly worship you and worthily magnify
your name,
through Jesus Christ our Lord, who taught us to pray,
saying,
Our Father. . . .

13

We lift our hearts to you, O God, after the rest of the night.
We thank you for the beauty of the day and the opportunity of coming to this place of worship. We pray for all who
are here with special needs today. May they experience
your presence and feel their burdens lightened. Help us to
worship you in spirit and in truth, through him who
instructed us to pray, saying, *Our Father. . . .*

14

An Opening Prayer for Advent

Lord, have you really been long expected, or is it part of
our problem that we have ceased to expect you at all? That
we don't expect you to intervene in our lives or help us
with our problems, or show us your will for our futures?
Renew our sense of expectation, we pray. Let the carols of
Christmas and the stories of your birth rekindle in us a feel-

ing for your role in our lives and for the difference you can make in our world. Through Jesus Christ our Lord. Amen.

15
An Opening Prayer for Advent

O God, whose nature is beyond finding out, yet who has revealed yourself in the child of Bethlehem, we come to you in praise and adoration for the gift of yourself to the world. We are deeply aware of the darkness around us—of hate and strife and envy and deceit and greed and selfish ambition. Therefore we are grateful for moments such as this, when we bow in your presence and know the hope of redemption. Tune our hearts to sing a new song this day—the song of your coming among us—and let it be heard in the lives of our families and friends and all those around us. Through Jesus, who was born in a stable, yet reigneth forever and ever. Amen.

16
An Opening Prayer for the Sunday After Christmas

The presents are opened, O God; the turkey is eaten and the eggnog is drunk. We thank you for the humanity of Christmas: for the excitement and the joy and the signs of warmth and kindness. But now, we come into your house and ask that the important things may be lasting: that the sense of the birth and incarnation may continue; that the feeling for Mystery may grow; that the delight in gift-giving may lead us to give ourselves to him whose birthday we have celebrated. We pray in his spirit, recalling the prayer he has taught us, saying, *Our Father. . . .*

17

We gather before you today, O God, as humble creatures who often lose their way, who become unhappy over insignificant setbacks, who make wrong choices and grumble at living with the consequences, who easily tire of well-doing, and who often live without noticing the beauty of our surroundings or the loving arms waiting to enfold us. Forgive us for our smallness and awkwardness, and teach us to have a sense of humor about ourselves. Grant that the ways of Jesus may become our ways, and that we may live with the kind of openness and awareness that always characterized his earthly life. To that end, hear us as we pray together, saying, *Our Father. . . .*

18
An Opening Prayer for Palm Sunday

In the excitement of this holy season, O Lord, we wave our palm branches and lay down our garments in the road, bidding you to enter and be present in our midst. Help us to open our hearts for your coming, and not to close them in fickleness when you make demands of us. Let this community of faith be yours, and let all who live in it this day experience new wholeness of heart and soul and body. For you have given us hope, and have taught us to pray, saying, *Our Father. . . .*

19

The world praises you, O God. The sun, the stars, and the moon praise you. The mountains and the seas praise you. The meadows and rivers praise you. The grass and the trees and the sky praise you. The birds and the fish and the animals praise you. Now let us, who above all created beings were made to worship and adore you, praise you through Jesus Christ our Lord, who taught us to pray, saying, *Our Father. . . .*

20

O God, who was there last evening in the comfort of our homes and the rest of the night, and is here now in the sound of church bells, the concourse of voices, the light streaming through colored windows, we praise you for your nearness and accessibility to all who seek you. Forgive the waywardness that has diverted us from a more steady awareness of you, and draw us back once more into the joy and comfort of your presence. Let your healing spirit repair our brokenness, our lack of trust, and our unbelief. Give us the renewed hope and confidence and enthusiasm we need to meet the demands of life today, and let us bind ourselves again to the duties of your people to seek justice, to love mercy, and to walk humbly in your presence. Through Jesus Christ our Lord. Amen.

21

O God, who shelters us in your love and then exposes us to the forked lightning of your judgment, receive us now tenderly and graciously as we approach you in worship. Some of us have been badly hurt in life. Some are bitter and resentful. Some are weak and fearful. All have sinned. Gather us up in your arms and heal our brokenness, that you may then instruct and lead us. Be gentle in your reproaches and magnanimous in your judgments, as it becomes you, through Jesus Christ our Lord, who taught us to pray, saying, *Our Father. . . .*

22

Blow now upon us, O God, the fresh wind of your spirit. Refresh our souls, that are weary from the world and its daily quota of crime and deceit and lack of hospitality. Help us to forget here for a little while the difficulties of ordinary existence and breathe from your presence new hope and new purpose and new direction for our lives. Embolden us to pray and seek your face, that everything else may find its proper place in the order of living. Through Christ our Lord. Amen.

23

Almighty God, unto whom all hearts are open and all desires known, we come before you today with singing and thanksgiving for the gift of life and faith. Only in you, O God, is there meaning for our suffering and hope for our sacrifice. Speak to our hearts as we wait before you, and let your Holy Spirit renew us in our inward parts, that we may serve you acceptably in our time and in our way. Through Jesus Christ our Lord. Amen.

24

We confess, O God, that we have not given you enough praise and glory in our lives. In our shortsightedness, we have thought more about ourselves and our welfare than about the world you have made, and the other people who live in it, and the joy we should take in simply being your children. Forgive us, we pray, and renew a right spirit within us. Teach us to live more abundantly by seeking less for ourselves and spending more of our time celebrating your wonderful presence in the world. For you are God, and we are your humble creatures, brought to this understanding through Jesus Christ our Lord, who taught us to pray, saying, *Our Father. . . .*

25

O God and Father of our Lord Jesus Christ, maker of the universe and giver of life, we lift our hearts in praise and thanksgiving for the light that awakened us this morning, the strength of will and limb that raised us from our beds, the beauty of the world that awaited us, and the inclination of spirit that brought us to this holy place. We confess to you the unworthiness of our lives and thoughts before your sacred presence, and pray that you will nevertheless draw near to us in love and mercy. Enable us to lay aside the things that hinder us from becoming whole and well.

Renew a right spirit within us, and make us followers of him who taught us how to pray, saying, *Our Father. . . .*

26
An Opening Prayer for Mother's Day or Father's Day

O God, whose presence we daily record in thousands of ways—in the abundance of our lives, in the songs of birds, in the joy of friends and children and extended families, in the work we enjoy doing and in the stimulation of our imaginations—we thank you for our faith and all who have helped to make it possible, whose witness to it in years gone by has kept it alive and meaningful for us today. We praise you, on this Mother's/Father's Day, for our own mothers/fathers, imperfect as some of them are or were, and for the memories of them that bring smiles and tears to our eyes. And we bless you for the life and insights of our Lord Jesus, who taught us to call you Father and to pray, when we undertake to pray together, saying, *Our Father. . . .*

27

O God, who has made yourself known in countless ways, by the glory of the sunrise and the sound of rain in the trees, by the beauty of flowers and the majesty of mountains, by the faces of people we love and the noises of children at play, by the words of prophets and psalmists and preachers, and most of all in Jesus Christ your eternal Son, we praise you for your self-revelation and for drawing near to us in love and forgiveness. Tune our spirits, in this hour, to turn in your direction, that our hopes may be renewed, our bodies healed, and our dreams amended, through that same Jesus Christ who taught us to pray, saying, *Our Father. . . .*

28

You have always been our help in ages past, O God, a steadying hand when we trembled, a solid rock when the waters rose about us. We praise you for the gift of your love, and for the many times you have come to our aid when we did not even realize we were in danger. You have saved us to this moment, and brought us together in this pleasant place to worship you. Crown your mercies with a strong sense of your holy presence, that we may leave here today in the assurance that you have once more touched our lives and made us whole, through Jesus Christ our Lord, who taught us to pray, saying, *Our Father. . . .*

29

The earth is indeed a beautiful place, O God, and we thank you for attuning our senses to it: for the breezes that stir the leaves on the trees; for the energy of cities and the peacefulness of the countryside; for the lovely flowers that draw our eyes to lawns and parks; for flashing rivers and awesome mountains; and for this stalwart church, where generations of the faithful have worshiped you. Grant us a sense of life and history, of past and present and future all caught up in your grand design, and help us to bow down in true contrition to adore you, through Jesus Christ our Lord, who taught us to pray, saying, *Our Father. . . .*

30

Your name is praised, O Lord, in all the lands of the earth and all the islands of the sea. We praise you for trees and birds and clouds and flowers. We praise you for the sounds of laughter and church bells and people singing. We praise you for the smiles on strangers' faces, the tender touch of friends, the rebirth of hope and joy in a place like this. Come among us with redemption and healing and renewal, and teach our hearts to pray truly the words our Lord Jesus has taught us to pray, saying, *Our Father. . . .*

31

An Opening Prayer for the Sunday Nearest Independence Day

Century after century, O God, you march on and on, your glory gathering about you like the lustrous train of a mighty robe! We praise you for your nation Israel, and for your chosen people the Church, and for all our forebears in the faith. We thank you for this country, conceived in godliness and devoted to freedom, and for the noble patriots' dreams that have become a model for democratic aspirations in all the world. Forgive our sins as a nation, and help us to rededicate ourselves to the great ideals of independence that continue to thrill our hearts and souls, through Jesus Christ our Lord, who taught us to pray, saying, *Our Father. . . .*

32

We are gathered here this morning, O God, from many homes and many neighborhoods to praise your name and renew our sense of commitment to you. It has been a busy week for most of us, and our hearts are filled and fluttering with many things—business, shopping, school, homemaking, travel, some hard and trying moments. Help us now to find the center of everything again, and having found it, to worship you in gladness and truth, realigning our hopes and desires, our plans and passions, our sentiments and understandings. Through Christ our Lord, who taught us to pray, saying, *Our Father. . . .*

33

You are indeed mighty in power, O God. You raised up the mountains and scooped out the ocean depths. You set the stars in their motion and brought forth life on this planet. You preside over the seasons of the year and the seasons of our lives. Yet you are also a God of love and care, who mourns our unresponsiveness and agonizes over the suffering of the smallest child in the remotest village of the world. Fill us now with your Spirit, that we may see life as it really is and not as our culture has told us it is. Help us to follow the life and ministry of Jesus in our own lives, that we may know with him the joy and power of the Resurrection. Instruct our hearts in tenderness and our souls in courage, that we may serve you well today and all our lives, through Jesus Christ our Lord, who taught us to pray, saying, *Our Father. . . .*

34

O God, who has made yourself known in a thousand ways, by the glory of the sunrise and the smell of rain on hot pavements, by the beauty of flowers and the grace of a bird in flight, by the faces of people we love and the noises of children at play, by the words of prophets and psalmists and preachers, and most of all in Jesus Christ your eternal Son, we praise you for your self-revelation and for drawing near to us in love and forgiveness. Tune our spirits in this hour to turn in your direction that our hopes may be renewed, our faith restored, our bodies healed, and our dreams amended, through that same Jesus Christ who taught us to pray, saying, *Our Father. . . .*

35

We thank you for the world of things bright and beautiful, O God—for woods and rocks and flower gardens; for seas and skies and lovely old houses; for people whose friendliness makes us smile; and for churches like this one, where worshipers gather to remember the past and dream of the future, to ask for forgiveness and enjoin compassion, to praise you in song and to feel renewed and encouraged in your presence. Give us the sensitivity to see the brightness and beauty at all times, and to value life for the wonderful gift it is, every day that we live. Speak to our hearts of the things we need to hear, and prepare us for your divine service, through Jesus our Lord, who taught us to pray, saying, *Our Father. . . .*

36

Your name is indeed glorious, O God, but for much more than the ordinary meaning of glory. You are glorious because you care about small things: about tiny flowers and little children and minor hurts and disappointments. It has always been your nature to be present in places where we have not thought to look for you: among the barren rocks, on bustling city streets, in lonely apartment buildings, in the hearts of those going through pain and disillusionment. Be present to us this morning in all these places, that what was stunted or broken in our lives may begin to heal and become whole again, through Christ Jesus our Lord, who taught us to pray, saying, *Our Father. . . .*

37

Sometimes, O God, we think our world has forgotten about holiness. Your law is broken, your name is used with disrespect, children don't honor their parents, and we worry that chaos is swallowing up our civilization. But then we remember the many good people we know, and the kindness in their hearts. We recall the delicacy of feeling expressed in certain poems and songs, and in the best books and movies. And we know that while the world is filled with crime and vileness and disregard, there are many who greatly cherish your name and your presence, and we give thanks for them. Teach us to care about everything and to spend our lives in pursuit of the goals and values that matter most to your kingdom. Show us love in the smile of a friend, tenderness in the regard of a little child, and glory in the beauty of a single flower. And we shall praise you forever through Christ our Lord, who taught us to pray, saying, *Our Father. . . .*

38

In the beauty and variety of the world around us, O God, we are reminded of your infinite creativity and generosity. You have lavished on us outward loveliness and inward peace and delight. You have filled us with a spirit of love and fellowship, and provided a beautiful place for our worship. You have given us the strength and will to be here. Our cups overflow, and we suspect that goodness and mercy shall follow us all the days of our lives. We thank you and praise you, in the name of our Lord Jesus Christ, who taught us to pray, saying, *Our Father. . . .*

39

There are many forms of beauty in your world, O God. One is the beauty of all these faces gathered in worship and expectation this morning. Make us aware of the beauty in one another, a beauty derived from you because you are our Lord, because you have made us and endowed us with your own features, your own desire to love and be loved. Let this be a time of true fellowship and deep meaning for us as we recognize and celebrate your presence in our midst, shining in our hearts and glowing on our faces, a presence that was made known so fully in Christ, who taught us to pray, saying, *Our Father. . . .*

40

We are grateful, O God, for the days when everything seems to go well and we feel good about life—days when we have our health and people are kind and our hearts are throbbing with love and joy. But we are also grateful that you are with us on the days when we don't feel so triumphant—when there is pain and loss and grief and suffering, when the skies are gloomy and we are unhappy with ourselves. We pray for each person in this sanctuary this morning, those who are in the triumph phase of life and those who are in the other; and we pray for our world, where many are joyful and many are miserable, deprived of the things they need. Let your spirit be upon all of us, that we may love one another and care for those who need things, and that we may praise your name through Christ our Lord, who taught us to pray, saying, *Our Father. . . .*

THREE

Affirmations of Faith

1

We believe that God is Spirit, and that those who worship
God must worship in spirit and in truth. We believe that
God is Light, and that if we walk in the light we have fel-
lowship with one another.
We believe that God is Love, and that everyone who loves
is born of God and knows God.
We believe that Jesus Christ is the Son of God and that in
him we have life now and forever.
We believe that as Christ loves us, so we must love one
another.
And we believe that salvation and glory and power belong
to our God, who reigns forever and ever. Amen.

2

We believe that God created the earth, and that everything
in the earth belongs to God.
We believe that God has given us this nation and blessed us
with freedom and plenty.
We believe that freedom and plenty carry certain responsibilities: that we are to love justice and mercy, and walk
humbly with our God; that we are to share our gifts with
those who have less, both in this nation and in other
nations; and that we are to live with gratitude, thanking
God for the divine favor we have received.
We believe, therefore, that we cannot fully celebrate our
independence without remembering at the same time

our dependence upon God and exalting God's name among the nations. There is no power like the power of God. Glory be to God! Amen.

3

I believe in the God
   who has shown us great love in Jesus Christ
   and continues to touch our lives
   in places of deepest need and highest aspiration.
I believe that God wants
   to touch the lives of all people
   and bring them to a sense of grace and joy,
   as God has done for me.
Therefore I believe in evangelism
   as the act of sharing God's good news
   with others, that they too
   may be healthy and happy in spirit.
I believe that our salvation
   is something we have together,
   and not apart,
   so that my witness to the goodness of God
   is as important to my being saved
   as it is to my neighbor's.
And I believe that the best time
   to begin my witnessing is today,
   when I remember all that the Lord
   has done for me! Amen.

4

I believe in God, whatever storms may rage about me. I believe God cares for me, as God cares for all people, and that God's love is for all time to come.
I believe in Christ, whatever the world may say about him; I believe his death atones for sin, and that he lives forevermore, present to all believers.

I believe in the Holy Spirit, however hard it is to understand such things; I believe the Spirit teaches, guides, and comforts me, and that it will lead me into the fullness of God.

I believe in the Church, whatever others may think about it; I believe it is still the fellowship of the faithful, and that it helps me to be conscious of God in the world.

I believe in the forgiveness of sins, even though I often live as if I didn't; I believe that God's forgiveness allows me to relax as myself, and that it helps me to be more generous about the sins of others.

I believe in the life everlasting, whatever science may think about it; I believe that this life is but the lower school for another, and that knowing this casts everything in a different light.

I believe in saying what I believe, however others may feel about it; I believe that knowing what one believes is important in this age, and that it helps me to keep my thinking in order at all times. Amen.

5

I believe in the God of little children, who creates them warm and tender in their mothers' wombs and bestows them as gifts millions of times each year, upon both rich and poor.

I believe in Jesus Christ, who said "Suffer the little children to come unto me," and in the kingdom he said would be comprised entirely of childlike beings.

I believe in the Holy Spirit of God that broods over the face of the deep, claiming this child and that for the service of God in all humanity, through art and music, science and industry, government and church, and a thousand other ways.

It is a rich world, alive with the potential of all its children waiting to transform our lives for the glory of Creator, Child, and Holy Spirit. Amen.

6

We believe in God, who sent the divine Son to die for our sins;

We believe in the Holy Spirit, who came upon the disciples in great power at Pentecost, producing excitement and devotion;

We believe that the same God still loves us, the same death of the Son still atones for our sins, and the same Spirit still comes upon us, changing the way we see things, inspiring our commitment, and leading us to share what we have for the care of the poor and the preaching of the gospel;

And we believe that some of us may experience the Spirit's presence today if we will only humble ourselves, and pray, and seek God's will for our lives while we are in this place; for God has already promised as much! Amen.

7

I believe in God, who created the world and filled it with awesome beauty.

I believe in Christ, whose resurrection has changed the way we look at life and death.

I believe in the Holy Spirit, whose presence enables me to sing and laugh at misfortunes.

I believe that God has manifested himself or herself in these three ways, and in many other ways besides, and that this manifestation continues wherever I am and whatever happens to me, as long as I have eyes to see and ears to hear.

And because I believe in God, I believe in prayer, which is the way I listen and hear God speaking, and the way I learn to serve God in the world.

I am here today in order to pray, and, when I have prayed, I believe that my life will be stronger, better, and more centered in God's will. Amen.

8

I believe in the God who made and owns the world, and in the Servant God sent to redeem the world, and in the Holy Spirit who is God's presence in the world today.

I believe that everything I have is really God's, given into my keeping for the good of the world.

I believe that I am expected to live spiritually in the world, dealing justly with all persons and contributing to the care of the poor and needy.

I believe that my own life and the lives of those I love will be blessed by my faithfulness in stewardship and my devotion to spiritual matters, for God rewards those who seek the welfare of others and a greater sense of the heavenly kingdom. Amen.

9

I believe in God as the final MYSTERY, whose thoughts are higher than our thoughts and whose ways are beyond human discernment;

I believe in religion as the attempt to understand, express, and worship that MYSTERY, so that people with different backgrounds will find different ways of embodying and serving it;

I believe in Jesus Christ as the most perfect incarnation of that MYSTERY, with the result that his teachings, his death on the cross, and his resurrection from the dead all speak to me in the most compelling manner about God's ways and God's wishes for me as a human being. As the Apostle said, we now know only in part, but someday we shall know even as we are known, and shall come face-to-face with the MYSTERY of God. I believe that that will be heaven, and, for the time being, that is all I need to know. Glory be to God, whose being is now shrouded in MYSTERY but has revealed enough of the divine nature in Christ to satisfy me until I know more! Amen.

10

I believe in God, whose care for rightness and goodness preserves the world from utter destruction, and who has promised us a new world beyond this one that will make all our struggles worthwhile;

I believe in Jesus Christ, who died to make the new world a reality and who in the triumph of his resurrection calls on us to spread the gospel of that new world;

I believe in the Holy Spirit of Christ, his presence among us now, who empowers us to live with dedication and sacrifice and love in the old world, helping it to become new;

I believe in the Church as the fellowship of Christ's followers, worshiping and learning, teaching and growing, until we have all taken upon ourselves the image of the Master and become his representatives in the world;

And I believe in coming together as we have today to sing praises, to humble ourselves in prayer and meditation, to listen to the Word, and to clasp one another in the warmth of fellowship as a foretaste of the new world that is coming through Jesus Christ our Lord. Amen.

11

An Affirmation of Faith for Mother's Day

I believe in Jesus Christ, the Son of the living God,
   who was born of the promise to a virgin named Mary.
I believe in the love Mary gave her Son,
   that caused her to follow him in his ministry
   and stand by his cross as he died.
I believe in the love of all mothers,
   and its importance in the lives of the children they bear.
   It is stronger than steel, softer than down,
   and more resilient than a green sapling in springtime.

It closes wounds, melts disappointments,
   and enables the weakest child to stand tall
   and straight in the midst of adversity.
I believe that this love, even at its best,
   is only the shadow love of God,
   a dark reflection of all that we can expect of the divine,
   both in this life and the next.
And I believe that one of the most beautiful sights in the
   world is a mother who lets this greater love flow through
   her to her child, blessing the world with the tenderness
   of her touch and the tears of her joy.
Thank God for mothers, and thank mothers for God!

12

An Affirmation of Faith for Mother's Day or Father's Day

We believe in God as Lord, King, and Father Almighty.
We believe that God is intended by the pronouns "he" and
   "him," and that our understandings of "him" have been
   conditioned by a patriarchal society.
We believe, now that we are more sensitive to such matters,
   that God has feminine qualities as well—
   that "he" has the caretaking nature of a woman
   and the tender, loving heart of a mother,
   and that if it were not for the accidents of society and
   history, "he" might have been called "she" instead of
   "he."
We believe that above all the humanness of our language
   and our attempts to describe the attributes of God,
   "he/she" is accepting of our worship and is working for
   our eternal salvation, for which we owe "him/her" our
   deepest gratitude and everlasting praise.
   "Father/Mother" God, we love you. Amen.

13

We believe in God, who created the world and all that is in it, including the men and women who are given dominion over earth and sea and sky.

We believe that God gave the uniquely begotten son, Jesus Christ,for the redemption of this world from sin and bondage and that all who trust and follow him find a quality of life that others are plainly missing.

We believe that the Holy Spirit of Christ is alive and active in the world, calling us to repentance and leading us to deeds of compassion and healing.

We believe that God intends us to use our minds and imaginations in the service of the divine kingdom, constructing new possibilities for the poor and offering new hope for the handicapped.

We believe there are no hidden clauses in the gospel: God loves us; God wants to love the world through us; and our only happiness as followers of Christ is to lay down our lives for others, that the divine purpose may be accomplished. Amen.

14

I believe in God, who created the world and is still creating.

I believe that God is the God of time—of the slender moments that slip through the hourglass and of all the incomprehensible eons that constitute eternity.

I believe that God has given us the years of our lives as a period of growth and testing, to prove ourselves more worthy of the life that is yet to come.

God does not measure worthiness as we do, in terms of wealth and power and the observance of niggling rules; but God measures it in terms of love and grace and generosity, and whether we have thankful spirits that recognize the gifts laid daily at our humble doorsteps.

I believe the gifts are there, and that I must learn to see, and seeing, to respond; for it moves me that the creator of the world would offer gifts to me. If God has time for me, then I must make time for God. Amen.

15
An Affirmation of Faith for Father's Day

We believe in God the Father Almighty, who made the world and the stars and the galaxies of space;
We believe God continues to care about what God has made, even as a father cares for those he has sired.
We believe God relates to us as a thoughtful and loving father, providing all we need to be happy in life and grateful in spirit;
We believe it is presently God's will that we remain in the world and promote justice and peace for all God's children, whoever they are and whatever the color of their skin;
And we believe God will bring us safely home when life is over, to dwell with him in the unity of heart and soul commended by Jesus who knew him intimately and said, "I and the Father are one." Amen.

16
An Affirmation of Faith for Advent

I believe in the spirit of Christmas, for it is the spirit of our Lord Jesus Christ, whose birth it celebrates;
I believe in the lights of Christmas, for they remind me of him who is the Light of the world;
I believe in the greenery of Christmas, for it symbolizes the eternal life of those in Christ;
I believe in giving gifts at Christmas, for it is in keeping with the greatest gift the world has ever known;
I believe in being childlike at Christmas, for Jesus said we must become as children to enter the kingdom of heaven;

And I believe in the angels' song about peace on earth among persons of good will, for when my will is good, as it is at Christmas, I feel a peace and joy in my heart that is unlike anything else in all the world. It *has* to be the peace and joy of God! Amen.

17

An Affirmation of Faith for Advent

I believe that Christmas is more than a time for parties and ornaments; it is a time for remembering Christ and the incarnation of God's love in human flesh.

I believe there are gifts more important than the ones under the Christmas tree, such as the things we teach our children, the way we share ourselves with friends, and the industry with which we set about reshaping the world in our time.

I believe that the finest carols are often sung by poorest voices, from hearts made warm by the wonder of the season.

I believe in the angels' message that we should not be afraid—that the Child of Bethlehem is able to overcome all anxieties and insecurities.

I believe in prayer and quietness as a way of appropriating Christmas—that if I wait in silence I will experience the presence of the One born in the stable, for he lives today as surely as he lived then.

I believe in going away from Christmas as the wise men went—"another way." I want to be different when these days are past—more centered, more thoughtful, more caring.

And I believe God will help me. Amen.

18
An Affirmation of Faith for Palm Sunday

We believe that the man who rode into Jerusalem on a donkey
is the Lord of all history and of every city that ever was.
We believe that he came to save us from our sin and to
restore us to the Father.
We believe that he was cruelly treated, put to death on a
cross, and buried in a borrowed tomb.
We believe that God raised him from the dead, and that he
became the first fruits of those who were asleep.
We believe that he is present in our midst today, comforting our sorrow, showing us the way to tomorrow, and
challenging us to life in the kingdom.
And we believe that the day will come when the entire
world will be his and he will reign in glory as the
Restorer of all that was separated from God, receiving
our love and praise forever and ever. Amen.

19
An Affirmation of Faith for Easter Sunday

I believe in the beauty of spring
that is known in windy skies, blossoming fruit trees,
waving jonquils, and sweet-smelling grass;
I believe in the warmth of a friendship
that is communicated in gentle eyes, a loving smile, a
fond touch of the hand, and an arm laid on the shoulder.
I believe in the power of Christ,
whose presence is felt in every season of the year,
but especially now, when life wells up everywhere and
folks feel a quickening in their souls because it is spring
and summer is on the way.
I believe Christ is somehow responsible for both spring and
friendship, and that the excitement I feel today is related
to the fact that he was dead

but is alive forevermore, not only in our memories but in
the truest kind of actuality.
I worship him by coming here, and say "Hallelujah! Christ
is alive, and in this very place!"

20

An Affirmation of Faith for Pentecost

We believe in God, who created the world, summoned the
nation of Israel, sent prophets among the people, and
gave the Divine Son to die for our sins.
We believe that God sent the Divine Spirit upon the church
at Pentecost, causing those who were present to enter a
new style of personal relationships and a new way of living in the world.
We believe in the importance of remembering these things,
that we too may live in daily awareness of whose we are
and to what ends we move.
We believe that when we recall the works of God in other
times we are helped to serve God in our own time.
We believe that when we remember Christ he lives among
us today, healing our brokenness, calling us to discipleship, and leading us to victory in the world.
We believe that remembering the past is the best guarantee
of a meaningful present and a joyful future.
Therefore we dare to say today "We remember," and to
commit ourselves once more to the God who gives us the
only life that is really worth remembering. Amen.

FOUR

Prayers of Confession

1

We have not loved you, O God, as you have loved us. We have been like children who accepted love without knowing its cost. Forgive us, we pray, for every act of betrayal, every failure to be kind, every gratification of self, and every blindness to the needs of others. Come and dwell in us with your spirit of generosity, that we may bless the world with what you have given us. For your name's sake. Amen.

2

You have given us many gifts, O God, and we have failed to thank you. We have envied the gifts of others and wished for what we do not have. We have eaten our food without tasting it and worn our clothes without noticing them. We have taken baths without remembering those who have no plumbing and greeted friends and loved ones without breathing a prayer for our relationships. We have used the resources of the earth with no thought to replacing them, and taken for granted that they would be there forever. Help us to live penitently and joyfully, through Jesus Christ our Lord. Amen.

3

We have not loved the world, O God, as we should. We have not forgiven our enemies seventy times seven. We have not gladly turned the other cheek when offended. We have not gone the second mile with most people, and with some not even the first. We have not befriended the stranger or spoken kindly of the foolish. Yet you have loved us with a steady and unchanging love. You have been generous to us far beyond our worth, and merciful when we deserved no mercy. Forgive us, we ask, for seeing the faults of others and not seeing our own. Receive us again as your followers, and teach us anew how to love and be loved. For yours is indeed the kingdom that will be forever. Amen.

4

We have sinned this week, O God, in word, thought, and deed. We have said things we ought not to have said and withheld praise when it should have been given. We have thought that which was unkind, unholy, and unprofitable, and we have failed to think the thoughts of love, peace, and righteousness your Spirit would have given us. We have been busy about many things that should not have occupied our time and have neglected to do those things that would have served others and pleased you. Therefore we condemn ourselves before you and ask that your grace and mercy be upon us, to forgive our sins, heal our brokenness, and return us unto ways that are profitable to your kingdom. Through Jesus Christ our Lord. Amen.

Leader: God's forgiveness is as everlasting as the ages.
People: **God's mercy is as wide as the seas.**
Leader: Surely God will forgive our iniquities.
People: **God will restore a right spirit within us. Amen.**

5

In the natural joys of the summertime, O God, we are inclined to forget the disciplines of the inner life. We do not pray as regularly as we ought, or meditate on your Word. We think about our own pleasures and are neglectful of the needs of others. We enjoy the bounty of summer gardens and the pleasure of outdoor grills without remembering the starving peoples of the world. Forgive us, O God, and turn us again to things of the Spirit, that we may justify the grace you have shown us in Jesus Christ. Amen.

Leader: God always hears the honest prayers of the community of faith.

People: **God cares for us as parents care for their children.**

Leader: God will have mercy upon us, and deal with us in loving-kindness.

People: **God will forgive our sin and restore us to a warm relationship. Amen.**

6

I think I am a pretty good person, O God, until I come into the sanctuary. Then I realize how many things are wrong in my life. Many of my values have been confused with the world's values. I have cared more about a good appearance than a pure heart. I have sought riches and security instead of treasures in heaven. I have desired the praise and admiration of others more than a "Well done, good and faithful servant" from you. Here in the community of faith, I recognize the emptiness of my life without you. Forgive me, O God, and help me to make it up to you. Let the meditations of my heart and the actions of my daily life become acceptable in your sight, O Lord, my strength and my Redeemer. Amen.

Leader: God is not a tyrant who desires our suffering and discomfort.

People: **God is a loving parent who wishes the best for us.**

Leader: God's desire for us is that we turn from our sin and discover the fullness of joy in Christ.

People: **God hears us when we pray, and restores us to newness of life.**

Leader: Therefore we praise God's name above every name.

People: **And give thanks for divine mercy. Amen.**

7

Almighty and everlasting God, who despises nothing you have made and forgives the sins of all who are penitent, create and make in us new and contrite hearts, that honestly lamenting our sins and acknowledging our shortcomings we may obtain of you perfect remission and forgiveness, through Christ our Redeemer. Save us from the blindness that keeps us from knowing we are sinning, the pride that prevents our admitting we are wrong, the self-righteousness that stops our seeing the flaws in ourselves, the callousness that prevents our caring, the defiance that keeps us from being sorry for what we've done, the evasion that always puts the blame on someone or something else, the heart that is so hardened it cannot repent. Give us a true sense of penitence and remorse in order that we may be truly forgiven, and find that your love is great enough to cover all our sin, through Jesus Christ. Amen.

8

O God, we confess to you that we have sinned and done that which was unworthy in your sight. We have gone our own ways and sought our own pleasure, instead of adhering to your way and seeking the welfare of others. We know that coming to church and appearing respectable in our community does not make everything all right with you. Forgive us, O God, and help us to be truly penitent. Let our faith be renewed in this hour, and our hearts turned again to your way. Through Jesus Christ, who died for us. Amen.

Leader: Christ died for us, the just for the unjust.

People: **In his blood is our peace.**

Leader: There are mysteries in this beyond understanding.

**People: God will heal our brokenness and set us in
the right direction.**

Leader: I assure you that God, for Christ's sake, has
forgiven us.

9

Almighty God, to whom all hearts are like open books, we
confess that we have fallen short of your will for us. We
have eaten our bread without concern for the hungry. We
have warmed ourselves without thinking of those who are
cold. We have prayed and enjoyed our faith without witnessing to those who do not know you. Forgive us, O God,
and bestow upon us the mind of Christ. Let us become sensitive to the needs of your world, and servants of all,
through Jesus our Lord. Amen.

Leader: Christ has sent his spirit upon us to lead us in
the way we should go.

**People: Our sins were forgiven when he died on the
cross.**

Leader: Now we are called to follow him in love and
sacrifice.

**People: God makes a community of those who take
up their crosses and follow him. Amen.**

10

We confess to you, O God, that we have not remembered
you enough this week. We have gone our own ways without being mindful of your presence. We have sought our
own welfare without thinking of others. We have neglected
your kingdom for the pursuit of our own desires in this
world. Forgive us, we pray, and turn us again to the
remembrance of things that matter. Let our commitment to
you become fresh and strong again. In Jesus' name. Amen.

Leader:	"If my people will humble themselves and pray," says God.
People:	**"Then I will hear from heaven and forgive their sins."**
Leader:	Surely God has heard our prayer and will pardon our sins.
People:	**God's mercy is everlasting and beyond all understanding.**
Leader:	Let all the people say, "Amen, so be it."
People:	**Amen, and so be it!**

11

I admit, O God, that I have not been zealous enough in my discipleship. I have not struggled to understand the great ideas of the faith, nor have I really attempted to give you the mastery of my life. I have lived selfishly in a world of misery and hunger, and have not sought to be Christ to my neighbor. Forgive me and help me to begin in this moment to be a new person in Christ. Let the love that is waiting for me in your arms redirect me in all my ways. Amen.

Leader:	God will not fail to fulfill all the divine promises.
People:	**God has promised to hear our prayers and forgive our sins.**
Leader:	Then our prayers are heard and we are forgiven.
People:	**We can begin again and live for God! Amen.**

12

We do not like to be reminded of our sin, O God; we prefer to think of ourselves as decent and good and easy to get along with. Yet when we are confronted by your holiness we know how inadequate we are, and how far short we fall. Forgive us, we pray, and teach us to live in constant remembrance of your glory. That way we shall keep our own lives in order and witness to your love and mercy, through Jesus Christ. Amen.

Leader: God has sent Christ to die for our sins, the righteous for the unrighteous, and God's forgiveness is free to all who call on the divine name in penitence and humility. For Christ's sake, you are forgiven and commended daily to seek God's will for your lives. Amen.

13

O God of light and shadow, we confess to you the shadowy side of our makeup. Our thoughts are often gloomy when they should be joyous. Our judgments of others are often grudging when they should be generous. Our sharing of self is often minor when it should be major. Our time for practicing your presence is often splintered when it should be whole. Forgive us for the darkness of our ways, we pray, and let the Light of the World shine in our hearts. For in your kingdom there is no dimness of spirit or shadow of doubt. Amen.

Leader: God has sent the divine Son to dispel our darkness.
People: In him there is light and life for all people.
Leader: He forgives our sin if we earnestly repent.
People: He restores us to the light, that we may walk uprightly and love goodness.
All: Blessed be the name of the Lord! Amen.

14

O God, whose love is forever, yet as new as this morning's paper, we confess to you that we have spent little time thinking about you this week. The affairs of each day have crowded you out, and we have been more concerned with selfish pleasures than with discovering your presence. As a result, we come here in less strength and excitement than we ought to feel. Lacking the awareness of unseen hosts in our midst, we are often bored with our worship. Forgive us, we pray, and renew our vision of you. Let this be a time of reshaping our lives and thoughts, that we may become the people you have called us to be. Through Jesus Christ our Lord. Amen.

> *Leader:* God is faithful and just, if we confess our sins, to forgive us.
> *People:* **God has heard us before and will hear us now.**
> *Leader:* God is ever ready to heal those who are of a broken and contrite heart.
> *People:* **Blessed are those whose spirits come before God.**

15

I am embarrassed to admit, O God, how seldom I have thanked you for the many gifts in my life. You have given me so much that I have learned not to notice. Forgive me, and teach me to see with new eyes. Help me to share with others out of my abundance. Then I will understand what it means to be part of the Body of Christ and the human community. Amen.

> *Leader:* It is in learning to say "I am sorry" that we begin to change.
> *People:* **It is in changing that we find new life and hope.**
> *Leader:* It is as we find new life and hope that we are able to change more.
> *People:* **Thus God give us in Christ the power to become new men and women.**
> *Leader:* And saying "I am sorry" leads to the power of Christ.

16

There is an arrogance about our flesh, O God, that inclines us to think better of ourselves than we ought. We see more easily in others the faults that hinder our own faith. We confuse need with humility, and think we are righteous when we are not really tempted. We feel good about ourselves when we are free from pain and worry. Forgive us for our indifference to you and to the peoples of the world for whom Christ died. Make us more sensitive to our spiritual shortcomings, that we may be motivated to serve you faithfully. Through Jesus Christ our Lord. Amen.

Leader: God has been long-suffering toward the sins of the world.

People: **God has forgiven us seventy times seven.**

Leader: God never despises the prayers of a contrite heart.

People: **God will hear and restore us to the heavenly fellowship, that we may serve that fellowship with newness of spirit! Amen.**

17

I have done a lot of running this week, O God, but much of it was not for you. I have run in a lot of circles because I failed to organize my days in prayer. I have run down a lot of dead end streets, because I was not following the Spirit's leadership. I have run in loneliness, because I was not running for love of others. I have run with a sense of heaviness, because I was running under my own power. Forgive me, O God, and help me to find the right track for my life. Let running become fun again, and let me praise you as I run. Through Jesus Christ, who is the greatest Runner of all. Amen.

Leader: God always hears the prayer of a sincere heart.

People: **We are sincere, Lord, help our insincerity.**

Leader: Surely God has forgiven our sins,
People: **And is moving among us even now to restore in us the true spirit of running. Amen.**

18

O God, who has shown us only love and forgiveness, we confess to you that we have not lived in the spirit of love this week. We have experienced envy, hate, and resentment. We have not turned the other cheek or walked the second mile. We have cared for our own interests and forgotten the interests of others. We are not worthy of your love, but we ask your forgiveness. Let the spirit of Christ be renewed in us, that we may be saved from our selfish ways. Amen.

Leader: If we are truly repentant, God hears our prayers and forgives our sins.
People: **God will take away our hearts of stone and give us hearts of flesh.**
Leader: For God is a good God,
People: **And the divine mercy is from everlasting to everlasting. Amen.**

19

We confess, O God, that we have failed to be the Body of Christ. We have lived our lives separately, without a sense of union. We have trusted in our own strength more than in yours. We have cared more about temporal things than about things eternal. We have been more concerned for propriety than for truth, and more anxious for our own welfare than for world justice. We have talked about the cross without suffering, and about love without loving. Forgive us, O God, and restore us to our mission in the world. Through Jesus our Lord. Amen.

Leader: Christ loved the church and gave himself for it.

People: **Therefore God will hear our prayers for ourselves as the church.**
Leader: God never despises the prayers of the faithful.
People: **In loving-kindness, God will heal our brokenness and make us into a true and everlasting community. Amen.**

20

We are not worthy, O God, to be called your sons and daughters. Our thoughts are not your thoughts and our ways are not your ways. We are more concerned about ourselves than about others. We think more about the economy than about your kingdom. We have not learned to relax in your presence and enjoy praying. In many ways we are still unredeemed, and have not discovered the deep joys of the Spirit. Forgive us, O God, and save us from our own darkness. Let the blood of Christ atone for all our sins, and the Spirit of Christ fall upon us like saving dew. Amen.

Leader: God's love is never deceptive.
People: **God has promised to redeem us from our sin.**
Leader: The divine promises are yea and amen.
People: **Surely God has heard our prayer and will answer us in our need. Amen.**

21

A Confession of Sin for Thanksgiving

On the eve of another Thanksgiving, O God, we praise you for the abundance of gifts surrounding our lives: for church and fellowship, for faith and friends, for food and families, for homes and jobs, for love and worship. We confess that we do not always live gratefully, and that we often take the bounty of life for granted. Forgive us, we pray, and make our spirits sensitive to your presence, which enriches everything. Through Jesus Christ. Amen.

Leader: A truly grateful spirit is also a humble spirit.

People: **God's Word says that a humble and contrite heart is always welcome.**

Leader: God forgives our sin and restores us to new life in Christ.

People: **Let us give thanks, for our Savior reigns! Amen.**

22

O God, whose Son came as a stranger in our midst, we confess that he is often still a stranger. We have ignored his living presence and left him to hang on the cross while we have pursued the games and goals that were more attractive to us. We have not followed him in simplicity of life and love, sharing what we have with those less fortunate than ourselves. Forgive us, O God, and make our hearts to be truly penitent, that we may enter into your kingdom and praise you in the name of our Savior. Amen.

Leader: God so loved the world that he gave his only begotten Son to die for our sin.

People: **It is not God's will that any should perish, but that all should have eternal life.**

Leader: Surely God will hear us when we pray, and will not send us away empty-handed.

People: **God will forgive our sin and restore us to heavenly fellowship. Blessed be the name of the Lord! Amen.**

23

A Confession of Sin for Advent

It is my sin, O God, that I have not kept Christmas all year. After last Christmas I went back to tending flocks, and have forgotten to adore him who was born in a stable. Having followed the star and found the Baby, I have not followed the cross and found the Savior. Teach me to enter into the deep mysteries of the season, and so find meaning and joy for my existence. Let the spirit of Jesus be born in me, that I may bring glad tidings of great joy to all the people in my life. For his kingdom's sake. Amen.

Leader: Jesus did not come into the world to condemn the world,

People: **But that the world through him might be saved.**

Leader: His life was given for the redemption of many.

People: **His blood atones for all our sin.**

Leader: I can assure you that God, for Christ's sake, has forgiven us.

People: **That is our special joy at Christmastime. Amen.**

24

A Confession of Sin for Advent

I am not ready, O God, for the coming of Christ into my life. There is much I am not prepared to surrender. I do not want to give up home or family or friends to follow him. I cherish my possessions, and do not choose to share them with others. I like being my own master, even though I do not manage it very well, and am reluctant to submit completely to your will. It would be a great favor to me if you would lead me out of my selfishness and into your love. For yours really is the kingdom and the power and the glory forever. Amen.

Leader: The coming of Christmas is a reminder of God's desire for all humanity.

People: **It recalls God's involvement in human history.**

Leader: It says that God really cares about us and for-gives our sins.

People: **It means that God will answer our prayers and save us from ourselves. Amen.**

25
A Confession of Sin for Christmas or the Sunday After Christmas

I confess, O Lord, that I have not adored you as I ought to have done this Christmas. My head has been too filled with other things to think of you constantly. Forgive me, Lord, and help me to adore you now. Receive me as you received the shepherds and wise men, and bless my life forever. Amen.

Leader: The gift of God is repentance and forgiveness.

People: **God will forgive the heart that is truly contrite.**

Leader: God's mercy is everlasting, and God's good-ness is forever.

People: **Surely God accepts our prayers and pardons our sins. The divine mercy is forever! Amen.**

26
A Confession of Sin for the Sunday After Christmas

Christmas has come and gone, O Lord; the greetings have been exchanged and the gifts have been opened. Yet for many of us there is something missing. To the degree that we have not waited before the manger and worshiped you, we feel an emptiness inside. The lights and tinsel and pack-ages are not enough. You are the center of Christmas, O Lord. Help us even now to hurry to Bethlehem , and to remember what it means that you have come in the flesh for our salvation. Amen.

Leader: There is no place that Christ may not be found, if we only call upon him.

People: **He has heard our confession and forgiven our sin.**

Leader: The song of the angels can still be heard today.

People: **There is peace among those who walk in his will. Amen.**

27

A Confession of Sin for New Year's Sunday

O God, we confess that we have failed you in the past. We have cared more about ourselves than about your world. We have sought our own comfort while others suffered. We have transgressed your holy laws. We have prayed too little, rejoiced too seldom, and given thanks too half-heartedly. Forgive us, O God, and help us to be different in the coming year. Let the ministry begun in your Son be continued in us, that the whole world may be converted to your ways. Through Jesus Christ our Lord. Amen.

Leader: Christ died for our sins, the godly for the ungodly.

People: **In him we have forgiveness for all our failures.**

Leader: God looks on the hearts of those who truly repent.

People: **God will hear our prayer and restore a right spirit within us. Amen.**

28

A Confession of Sin for New Year's Sunday

As we begin a new year, O God, we confess our sin in the year that is past. We have often sought our own welfare and not the welfare of others. We have complained about the state of the world while doing little to change it. We have spent time worrying and talking that should have been spent praying and listening. We have invested energy in our appearances that should have been invested in the renewal of our hearts. Forgive us, we pray, and make new persons of us in Christ Jesus. Let the new year be what the old year should have been. For your name's sake. Amen.

Leader: God invariably hears the prayers of honest hearts.

People: **God is always present to those who call on the divine presence.**

Leader: God will see our humility and accept our repentance.

People: **God will renew our spirits within us, even as we have been promised. Amen.**

29
A Confession of Sin for Palm Sunday

We have laid our coats in the road for you, O Christ, that you might ride in triumph. Then we have taken them back again and denied even knowing you. We have turned on you in small ways, choosing what was good for us instead of what was good for the community. We have permitted you to be crucified by refusing to side with the right or speak out in your behalf. Forgive us, O Christ, and visit us again with your Spirit. Renew our lives by your presence and send us forth once more to live for you. Amen.

Leader: After the Resurrection, Jesus renewed the discipleship of Peter.

People: **Peter had failed Jesus even as we have.**

Leader: "Peter," said Jesus, "do you love me?"

People: **"Yes, Lord," said Peter, "you know that I love you."**

Leader: "Then feed my sheep," said Jesus.
People: Thus he restores us all, if only we love him. Amen.

30

A Confession of Sin for Easter Sunday

We confess, O God, that we have not lived each day in the faith of Easter. We have been like the disciples, who saw life more in terms of the suffering of Calvary than in terms of the Resurrection that followed. Forgive our doubt and despair, and help us to be more positive about life. Let the power and radiance of Easter morning transform us into new creatures in Christ, who get up every morning with the feeling that something wonderful is going to happen because our Savior lives! Amen.

Leader: As God raised Jesus from the dead, so God lifts us all from the graves of broken dreams.
People: God forgives us and translates us from sin to righteousness.
Leader: God makes the blind to see and the lame to walk.
People: God makes us whole again, and sends us forth to witness to our faith. Glory be to God! Amen.

31

O God of love and mercy, we confess that we often fail to love those who do not care for us. O God of righteousness, we admit that we often fall short of the goodness we wish we had. O God of all creation, we acknowledge that we often imitate others instead of trying to be creative or original. O God whose ways and thoughts are higher than ours, we bow our heads and confess our need of you.

Forgive us and heal us, and help us to praise you, through Christ our Lord. Amen.

Leader: It was an act of everlasting mercy that God sent Christ to die on the cross.

People: **He died for our sins, and by his death we are made whole.**

Leader: It is a great mystery, but God loves us and forgives us.

People: **Now we can praise God with hearts filled with gratitude! Amen.**

FIVE

Offertory Prayers

1

You have given us all that a wealthy parent could give his or her children, O God, of homes and food and loved ones and work and well-being. Now give us the gift of gratitude, that we may see all your goodness and be moved to share what we have with the poor and broken and neglected of the world, through Christ our Redeemer. Amen.

2

Great is the mercy you have shown us, O God. Great is the kingdom we have inherited in Christ Jesus. Great is the need of the world around us. Now let us respond to the mercy and the kingdom and the need with the greatest of generosities, that even our own lives will be changed in giving. Through him who loved us, even Christ Jesus our Lord. Amen.

3

To be gifted is one of the greatest joys of our existence, O God. Therefore we ask that you will receive these gifts of ours as a joy for you, realizing we are but children not yet capable of giving the gifts we shall one day give you, when we are joined with all the saints and angels in heavenly praise. Amen.

4

Forgive us, O God, for every time we have accepted anything from you thoughtlessly, or foolishly used it without considering your glory or the welfare of others, and enable us to present these offerings with love and sincerity, because you are our God and we are your grateful people. Amen.

5

Our gifts appear so small, O God, before One who has given us so much. But like children's gifts to their parents, let them be presented with all our hearts and enthusiasm, and thus be found pleasing in your sight, through Christ our Lord. Amen.

6

You astonish us each day, O God, with the boundlessness of your love and generosity. If there is one thing we learn in worship, let it be not to take any gift for granted, but to remember that it comes from you and to live in perpetual gratitude, through Jesus Christ our Lord. Amen.

7

It is a blessing to be able to give, O God, and we thank you for our ability. Help us in all our dealings, with other persons as well as with you, to become more and more generous, in order that we may be more like you and honor you by our behavior. Through Jesus, who was the most generous of men. Amen.

8

All blessings do indeed flow from you, O God, and there are no words to describe the greatness of your generosity toward us. Forgive us for any times when we have felt deprived or neglected, and remind us of the true immensity of our indebtedness to you, that we may always live as your grateful sons and daughters, through Jesus Christ our Lord. Amen.

9

We read in the Bible, O God, that you love a cheerful giver. It is also true that a cheerful giver is more likely to love you. Therefore teach us to share what we have with others and to make our offerings with grateful spirits. Through Jesus, who always gave everything. Amen.

10

The cattle on a thousand hills are yours, O God, and the diamonds in a thousand mines and the oil in a thousand wells. So are the homes we live in and the land we live on and the income with which we buy our food. We thank you for what we have by sharing it now with others in the world, through the work and ministry of this church and your kingdom. Amen.

11

Our lives are filled with your gifts, O God: the gift of life itself, the gift of friends and loved ones, the gift of home and food, the gift of daily work to do. There is nothing we can give you that compares with what you have already given us in Christ Jesus. But help us to give you the best thing we have, ourselves, and with them to share the good things you have given for the sake of others. Through Jesus Christ. Amen.

12

O God, we cannot begin to count all you have done for us. You have given us eternal life in Jesus Christ. You have set us in a world of plenty. You have given us this community of loving relationships. Now grant that what we have received may make us truly thankful, so that our gifts to you may be from the heart and not merely from the pocket-book or the checkbook. Amen.

13

There is no way, O God, that we can repay you for what you have done for us in Jesus Christ, or what you continue to do for us day by day. Our gifts are but the tokens of children to a parent, to say, "We love you, God." Amen.

14

O God, who gives and gives until some of us have no place to put everything we have, we apologize to you for being the people who have most on earth; and now we bring a part of what we have to lay it on the altar for the gospel and for the poor of the world, and ask you to receive it because we love you. Amen.

15

An Offertory Prayer for Advent

This is a season of giving, O God. Many of us will be in the spirit of giving and will give a great deal to persons and causes around us. And yet, if we do not give ourselves to you, our gifts are empty and void of meaning. Help us now, as we gather around the table that represents your ultimate gift to us, to open our lives to you and worship you fully, through Jesus Christ our Lord. Amen.

16

We tremble, O God, to think seriously of what we do at this time. We are bringing our gifts to you, who has given us everything, including the life of your only begotten. It is an awesome, frightening thing to do. Let our spirits praise you in this expression of our love and regard. Amen.

17

There is nothing in our hands, O God, that was not given by you. The earth, the seas, our homes, our incomes, the people we love, were all yours before they were ours. Therefore we can give you nothing that is not already yours, except our hearts. We come now to give them, and all in our lives that goes with them. Receive them and bless them, we pray, that your kingdom may rejoice and prosper in the world. Amen.

18

Lord, we remember before this table the poor and hungry of the world, and worship you now by sharing what we have with them. Take our gifts and give them wings to bring hope to a weary world. Through Christ, who commanded us to love one another. Amen.

19

An Offertory Prayer for Thanksgiving Sunday

In this season of thanksgiving, O God, we remember all your gifts to us, especially the gift of your Son who died to save us from our sin. May his name be exalted through this offering as it finds its way to many parts of the world, slaking thirst, assuaging hunger, healing sickness, and filling the souls of those who wait to hear your Word. Amen.

20

Our lives are filled with the sunshine of your love, dear God—with love and joy and gifts beyond all naming. Behold now as we share the sunshine with others, giving of our souls and substance to help those who live in darkness both here and around the world. We remember our missionary friends on other continents as they share themselves in an even more ultimate way, and ask that your name may be exalted and glorified, through them and us and Christ our Savior. Amen.

21

We bring our gifts, O God, in imitation of your many gifts to us, of life and food and shelter and friendship, and worship you for the unspeakable goodness of your spirit. Through Jesus Christ. Amen.

22

There are so many gifts here today, O God, of love and music and presence and encouragement, that the money we have put in the offering plates may seem small and inconsequential beside them. But bless it, we pray, like the loaves and fishes of old, that it my multiply and nourish the lives of many. Through Christ our Lord. Amen.

23

O God, who gives and gives until some of us have no place to put everything we have received, we apologize for being the people who have most on earth, and we bring a part of what we have to say thank you, and to offer ourselves for the battle for truth and goodness and justice in the world. Through Jesus Christ our Lord. Amen.

24

Teach us how to give, O God, as you give, openly, freely, generously, and then to find, as we always do, that you have replenished what was given, and more besides; for your openness, freedom, and generosity are far more than we have any right to expect, and we thank you, through Christ our Lord. Amen.

25

We are grateful for life, O God, and all the things that make it so rich for us. Help us to discover how rich it truly is by living in daily gratitude for everything, and then by sharing it with others. Through Christ our Lord. Amen.

26

When we look around us, O Lord, at the world of trees and flowers and loving friends, we realize we live each day with heavenly grace. Now we bow before the throne of all that grace to say thank you, Lord, for the constancy of your love, and to ask that we may be half as faithful in caring for those around us, whose world may not appear as heavenly as ours. Through Christ our Lord. Amen.

27

Gratitude is such a poor thing, O Lord, with which to repay the incredible outpouring of all your gifts to us. But to be ungrateful is even worse, for it stunts our souls. Therefore we ask for grateful hearts to appreciate what you have given us, that we may live our days in joyful contemplating of your graciousness and your wonder, and that we may sing even on the darkest days. Through Jesus Christ our Savior. Amen.

28

We are surely the most gifted people in all the world, O God, with too much to eat and too many rooms in our houses and too many things in our closets. Remind us of others who have so little, and in the shock of gratitude let us begin to care for them with what you have entrusted to us. Through Christ Jesus our Lord. Amen.

29

What can we say, O God, but thank you for the countless blessings of our lives. We are so rich, in a world that knows such great poverty, that we are compelled to worship you with all we have. Through Jesus Christ our Savior. Amen.

30

It is a pleasure to give to you, O God, who has given so much to us. As our Lord Christ blessed the loaves and fishes beside the sea and fed a multitude, we ask you to bless this offering that it may prove helpful to many, many people, here and to the uttermost parts of the world. Through Christ our Savior. Amen.

SIX

Pastoral Prayers

1

O God, whose being casts a bright shadow over all we think and do and are, we thank you for the world you have made: for blue skies and green meadows; for pinwheels and pollywogs; for feather pillows and lily ponds; for spiced tea and sparrows' nests; for poster beds and china bells; for windy days and whippoorwills; for taste of bread and gift of song. Forgive us for seeing so little, hearing so little, and loving so little. Teach us to live each day on tip-toe, anxious for the mysteries you will show us, grateful for the richness of life's tapestry. Grant peace to troubled hearts and hope to minds downcast. Give healing to the sick, comfort to the lonely, and joy to the mourning. Let the vision of your heavenly rule so fill our thoughts each day that we see it here on earth and share what we have with the poor, make friends of enemies, and celebrate the name of Christ wherever we go, with a singing and merry spirit! Amen.

2

O God, who watches over us with endless love and care, we thank you for the journey of life and each of its stages: for childhood, with its sense of wonder and discovery; for adolescence, with its miracle of growth and new relation-ships; for young adulthood, with its promise and chal-lenge; for midlife, with its sobering retrospectives and adaptations; and for later years, with their joy and fulfillment and even their new beginnings. It is all a rainbow of splendor and excitement, a pilgrimage of learning and experience. Help us to walk in it always with a sense of your presence, of never being alone, of living forever under grace. Teach us to rise above our mistakes, to forgive our enemies, to cherish friends, to love adventure. Inspire us to live to the fullest, both individually and in community. Let the talents and wisdom and love you have given us find rich expression in our work and play and daily relationships. Show us how to give ourselves to others until we have overcome the deficiencies in ourselves. Let goodness, mercy, and peace attend us all our days, and bring us at last into the presence of all your saints and angels, and of our Lord Jesus Christ, to whom be glory forever and ever. Amen.

3

We often come to this moment, O God, with little expectancy. It is another routine moment in the liturgy, something we have done dozens, even hundreds, of times. We do not begin to be aware of the tremendous power we are addressing, or of the desire you have to destroy the thin walls that divide us from yourself and come rushing upon us with all your love and strength and holiness. How radical a thing it is truly to pray, and how seldom we really do it. Show us how, dear God! Teach us to wait before you with hearts so open, with wills so ready to be made yours, that this time is never routine or dull or uneventful. Imbue us with your Holy Spirit, that will sweep us out of ourselves and our usual ways of perceiving the world and deposit us in completely new places for viewing our lives and our gifts and the people who surround us on this earth. Show us the possibilities that lie in our hands, in our possessions, in our corporate power and influence, to change the way people live and the very way the earth is governed. Free us from the lethargy that binds us like ropes and chains and graveclothes. Stir us to devotion and to action. Enable us to take arms against what the apostle Paul called "the powers of the air"—against hunger and poverty and prejudice and injustice and sickness and death and evil. Lead us victoriously out of our paralyzing preoccupation with pain and self and weakness, and reveal through us the triumphant power of your Word and your resurrection. And let us never, never pretend that we are praying when we are not, lest we offend your holiness and your love. Through Jesus Christ our Lord. Amen.

4

O God, who reveals yourself in the beauty of these golden days of autumn, but who will still be with us in the gray, cold days of winter, we celebrate your constancy. In a world where everything seems to be changing almost daily, you are always the same with us. Your arms are warm and glorious. Teach us to rely less upon ourselves and more upon you. Incline our hearts to your salvation, and to following in the way of your Son, Jesus. Reveal to us the emptiness of life when it is not built upon the foundation of your wisdom. Redeem us from our false dreams, our idols, and our selfish desires. Anoint our sick with your healing spirit. Comfort our friends who grieve at the loss of loved ones. Guide the leaders of our nation into pathways both sane and bold. Instill in us a devotion to the poor and hungry of the world. Make us generous and gracious and caring. Let our stewardship of life be acceptable in your sight. Keep us from thoughts and deeds that would debase our lives, and strengthen us for living truly and making sacrifices to love. Lift us now on the wings of worship, that we may exult in your presence and then return to our daily existence transformed and reinvigorated. Through Jesus Christ our Savior. Amen.

5

There are so many things we would like to have made new today, O God. Some of us would like to have our health made new—to be young and strong and vigorous again. Some of us would like to have our love made new—to care for others the way we once did, and to feel that they care for us as they did. Some of us would like to have our faith made new—to believe as we once believed, and to feel the energizing power of that belief extending into everything we do and are. Some of us would like to have our hope made new—to expect that good things are going to happen and we are going to be rewarded by the future. Some of us would like to have our opportunities made new—to be able to start over in our jobs, in school, in our marriages, in the church, with our children or our parents, and do things differently this time. You are the God of all newness, Lord. You are the One who makes all things new—even a new heaven and a new earth. Set newness in our hearts, O God—new health, new love, new faith, new hope, new visions of our opportunities. Show us what it is to be born again, this time from above. Anoint us with your Spirit's power. Lead us out of our old ways. Save us from the death of everything grown old and cold and repetitious. Give us life in your Son and let us share it with the world. For his name's sake. Amen.

6

In a moment of madness, O God, we gave ourselves to you. It was a moment of *divine* madness, that changed our lives. Now we spend all our days looking for such moments again, hoping to confirm what we felt before or to discover new creations of what it means to follow you. Therefore we pray for a special feeling of your presence now in our midst as we worship, that when we go from this place it will be with new courage, and with hope that our experience of you does order life and give it meaning beyond the momentary pleasures and sorrows of daily existence. From whatever vantage point we address you—from the grief of the newly bereaved, from the confusion of adolescence, from the weariness of age, from the disappointment of the rejected, from the confidence of the successful—let us have a sense of spiritual reality that overwhelms all other realities in this hour. Lift us, woo us, illumine us, inspire us. Make us new creates for having been here, and for having heard your Word, and for having sung your praises, and for having had this experience together. Let the whole world be different for what we have felt. Convert our gifts—and us—into living sacrifices that will make the poor rejoice, the wounded heal, and the lonely discover love. And let all our moments become moments of such madness. Through the One who died on a cross and was raised to newness of life, even Christ our Lord. Amen.

7

O God, who is known in heartbreak and in hope, and who has made yourself known in a Son, make him known to us now in the Spirit that fills this room. Let his personality overwhelm everything else, moving up and down these aisles, touching this person and that, and calling us all into discipleship. Let his teachings reverberate in our hearts and minds, inviting us to come and follow him. Let the image of his dying, the sound of nails driven into his hands, the thud of a cross lifted and dropped into the ground, the groaning of a man swimming upstream to death, be recreated so vividly in our memories that we take new allegiance to his kingdom. And let the vitality of his Resurrection, that makes all things new, like a garden of innocence, sweep in upon the pale shadows of our lives to remake us in his image, with his life, and his dreams, and his purpose. Forgive the lackluster and haphazard kind of commitment that has allowed your church to languish, and put us in touch with him, that together we may convert communities and nations to your way. Anoint the sick with your healing power, the young with your wisdom, the enthusiastic with your patience, and the tired with your energy. Teach us to pray and to witness and to care. And above all things, help us to wait on you, that we may not overrun life and miss its deepest meaning. Through Jesus Christ our Lord. Amen.

8

In the cool of the morning, O God, we praise you for the Creation: for hills tinged with autumn, for skies filled with birds, for lakes deep and cold, for late-summer gardens with their colored quiltwork of tomatoes and squash and corn and melons, for our own bodies sensitively tuned to changes in weather and the importance of sleep and exercise. Even now, as we wait before you in this place of worship, we are aware of our hearts pumping blood, our lungs taking in oxygen, our miraculous hands that perform countless tasks each day, our feet straining against the confinement of leather and lace. You have made the world most cunningly, O God, and you have made us most beautifully. Forgive us for the mistakes we have introduced into your creation: for pollution in streams and sky; for ghettos of despair in our cities; for injustices in our dealings with one another; for stress in our bodies; for anxieties in our minds. Grant, as we worship you, that beauty and goodness and truth may once more triumph in our lives, and the presence of Christ transform us into the noble men and women and boys and girls you planned for your world. Let all that is unworthy dissolve before your feet, and all that is righteous remain to praise you. Give peace and health and love, in the name of him who has been with you from the creation of everything, even Jesus our Lord. Amen.

9

We confess, O God, that we do not suffer well. When we have pain, we think it is the greatest ever felt; when we have hurts, we believe them the deepest; when we experience sorrow, the whole world begins and ends in us. We forget, O God, what pain you must feel. Your heart is so much bigger than ours, your care so much deeper. You see so much more than we see—the hunger and disease and burdens of all your people, all your little ones around the entire earth. How do you stand it, dear God? How can your heart bear what you know and feel? Teach us to remember your pain, that our own may be put in perspective. Help us to care about the things you care about and to love those whom you love. Let us share your pain and sorrow for the world until our own pains and sorrows have faded into nothingness. Grant that your little ones may become free, and your sick ones well, and your blind ones gifted with sight. Then we too shall be free and well and able to see, and we shall join them in praising you for your goodness and righteousness, through Jesus Christ our Lord. Amen.

10

O God, who commanded the angel that stirred the healing waters of Bethzatha, we need healing in our time as well. Like the poor man who lay by the pool, some of us need healing in our bodies. There are many illnesses and infirmities among us. Some of us need relief from distress of mind or soul—from anxieties and worries over which we have little control—from fears that we will not do well or will not be liked—from doubts about our abilities and our futures—from misgivings about our jobs or our relationships or our places in life. Send your angel again, dear God, and stir the waters once more. Let the love and power that were in Jesus Christ envelop us as in a special balm, that miracles may take place and we may learn to praise you with our whole hearts. Most of all, convert us in our inner beings, that we may care about our relationship to you, and that all life may center on that caring. "Naught be all else" to us, Lord, "save that thou art." And let this healing go out from us to the sick and worried world around us, that politicians may become whole, that the rulers of the nations may work for the welfare of the least of their peoples, that caring may take the place of competition, that greed and graft may disappear, that the elderly may be safe in their homes and little children may grow up in gentleness and joy, that the ever-present specter of war may give way to unmistakable signs of peace, and that the gospel of our Christ may sound in everyone's ears as wonderful words of life, to be sung over and over again, until all the earth rings with the glory of your presence, and the bear eats straw with the ox, and the lion and the lamb lie down together in the kingdom for which we were made. Through Jesus Christ our Lord. Amen.

11

O God, who loves us when we are at our worst—when we have broken the rules of life, when we have injured our health, when we have mistreated our friends and families, when we have hated ourselves and complained about you—teach us how to love with your love. Let us begin by caring for ourselves—for our health, for our spirits, for our welfare, and for our joy. Then, out of the fullness of the self, let us reach out to others, caring for their health and spirits and welfare and joy. Show us how the death and Resurrection of Christ are related to all of this—to forgiveness of our sins and fullness of life and the desire to follow him by giving ourselves for others. And grant, O God, that leaving behind the old self and all its negativism, we may rise to newness of life in you, so that we see and feel and taste and hear the wonders of our existence in the world, and live in excitement and gratitude and humility. Through Jesus Christ our Lord. Amen.

12
A Pastoral Prayer for Mother's Day

We pray, O God, for all the mothers of the earth: for mothers who are young and only beginning the way of motherhood, that they may be imbued with patience, love, and wisdom; for mothers who are older and have found the way hard, that they may be given renewed strength and love and courage; for mothers whose children are encumbered with unusual difficulties, that they may bear the pain of being unable to make everything all right for the ones they love; for mothers whose children do not have enough food to eat, or medication for illness, that they may not lose hope; for mothers whose children have died, that they may expect a joyous and fulfilling reunion beyond this life; for mothers whose children have been given for adoption, that they may trust in your love and watchfulness over these extensions of themselves; for mothers-in-heart, who have been unable to bear children, that their motherly instincts may be fulfilled by caring for significant others in their lives. We bless all mothers, dear God, for their part in your plan for the world, and for the tenderness and caring which they have bestowed upon our existence. Quicken in all of us, males and females alike, a mothering spirit toward one another, gentle, loving, and full of grace, and we shall praise you forever and ever, through Christ our Savior. Amen.

13

O God, who hears the prayer of the smallest child and the most wayward adult, hear now the murmurings of our hearts. We pray for light in our darkness, that our minds may be illumined and drawn into service for you. We pray for rest from our fevered existences, that we may experience your peace and be changed from our fretful ways. We pray for the capacity to feel your great love for us, that we may be no longer lonely or fearful, and that your spirit of health and vigor may flow through us to the needy world around us. Take from us meanness and pride and envy, that we may look upon the world joyfully and excitedly, cherishing the welfare and happiness of others even above our own. Teach us to wait with you day by day in quiet ways until your spirit forms itself in us, and we are not our own but yours who came to us in the life and death and resurrection of Jesus. Give to our world, we pray, a greater capacity for peace, and to our leaders the humility to bow themselves before the throne of grace. Let industrialists care about the peoples of developing nations, let those of us who live in plenty reach out to those who live in desperation, let the architects of the future cherish the little ones who cannot pay, and let the kingdoms of this world become the kingdom of our Christ, that we may praise you forever and ever, in his blessed name. Amen.

14

You are there, O God, even when we are unaware of you. You touch our lives with grace in a thousand ways: with the smiles of people we pass, the gurgling sounds of babies, the flowers growing where we didn't expect them, the taste of hot bread, the sight of a hawk sailing in a clear blue sky, the rustle of leaves, a letter from someone we love, the warmth of a friend's voice, the security of a favorite room in the house, the view from a window, the comfort of an old pair of shoes. How manifold are your gifts, O God, and how seldom we praise you. Teach us to see with new eyes the wonders through which we move. Make children of us, for whom the world is vibrant with color and texture. Take away our weariness, our habit of not being present, our dullness to what is beautiful and holy. Make us sensitive to people, and to where you are moving in their lives. Show us how to celebrate the Resurrection. Through Jesus Christ our Lord. Amen.

15

O God, whose mystery is like the surface of deep water, reflecting the face of the one who seeks you, we bow before you in reverence and humility. We have heard your name since we were small children. We have discussed you as we have discussed the weather. In the marketplace, we have spoken casually of our relationship to you. But for all that, we have not really known you. You continue to evade us, to rise above our definitions, to elude our search. Always when we fall upon some aspect of your being and think we have you at last, you evaporate like mist in a jar and we are left with our empty containers. Only in Jesus have you revealed yourself in a way we can understand. Only in his love for the disciples do we begin to know the love you have for us. Only in his teachings do we perceive what it is that we must do. Only in his death do we see the limits to which we must go. Only in his Resurrection do we glimpse the life that is promised to us. Keep us faithful to these understandings, that we may remain in covenant with you. Let the power that is in them give effectiveness to our living. And let the gifts that are in us become gifts for the world around us. For yours is the kingdom, the power, and the glory. Amen.

16

Almighty God, whose holiness is so great that we would not dare to approach you were it not for the audacity of your gift to us in Jesus Christ, we open our hearts to you this morning in all our variety of needs and moods. Some of us are in pain. Some are confused. Some are tired. And some are radiantly happy. We thank you that you meet us where we are, that you have always come to us where we are. Receive especially, we pray, the brokenhearted and troubled among us. Give comfort where there is grief, and courage where there is fear. Replace desperation with hope and sickness with health. Let your light shine into the darkness of our problems, illumining our situations and helping us to see beyond the immediate horizon of our small beliefs and limited understandings. Make us grateful for the deep and good relationships of our lives—for wives and husbands, for children and parents, for friends and relatives. Help us so to live that we make none of them ashamed of us and never abuse their love or trust. In all things grant us your Spirit, that we may live better than it is in us to do, and that we may walk faithfully with Christ even when doubts and temptations beset us. For you are our God, and yours are the words of eternal life. Amen.

17

O God, whose love is from everlasting to everlasting, yet very particular in this moment, we thank you for the world of our senses this morning: for the sound of birds singing as we arose, for the smell of fresh coffee perking in the pot, for the views of trees and grass around our homes, for the touch of loved ones after sleeping, for the taste of food on our tongues, for the mingled familiarity and strangeness of the streets we traveled to come here, for the chorus of voices in the halls, for the magnificence of the organ, the presence of others in the pews, the awareness of something special in this place. Now let all of that fade away, that we may feel your presence most of all, and know that all else has meaning because of you. Having created the world, you have entered it to redeem it through Jesus Christ. Our hope is in him and his dream for the world as your kingdom. Help us now, trusting in him, to surrender all our problems. Let us rely not upon ourselves but upon you, that your power and justice may flow through us, healing us, redirecting us, and exciting us. We commit to you all those who are heavyhearted, all who languish through illness, all who feel confusion or fear or loneliness. Speak to us now through your Word, that the world of our senses may become even more vivid and compelling. Through him who saw transcendence even in the ordinary dimensions of life, namely our Lord Jesus Christ. Amen.

18

This is your world, O God, that glows with the radiance of bursting flowers and blooming trees, with the warmth of human care and kindness. But there is another world that is yours as well: a world of brokenness and barrenness, of sickness and isolation, of suffering and loneliness, of twistedness and dementia. We thank you, O God, that you have owned not only the beautiful world, but the world of ugliness and sin as well. It was the world of ugliness and sin that Christ died to redeem. It was to this world, not the other, that the cross reached out its arms. Receive us, we pray, from the darker and needier side of our existence this morning. Let the hurt and resentment in us be taken up into your love and acceptance. Let our loneliness be assuaged by your presence. Let our illness be touched by your health, and our troubled spirits by your peace. Turn our personal worlds of suffering and confusion into the world of Christ, where all things are seen differently in the light of his wonderful face. And grant that the conversion of our own worlds will enable us to care about the worlds of others—the poor, the hungry, the broken-spirited, the sick, the dying, the illiterate, the disenfranchised, and the imprisoned. Save us from ever thinking that the beautiful world we live in is ours, or that the broken and lonely world we live in is the only one there is. Keep ever before us the vision of the cross, by which the two worlds are united, and the spirit of the Resurrection, in which we are promised that the beautiful world will survive the broken one. Through Jesus Christ our Lord. Amen.

19

O God, who is an infinite care that nothing be lost or neglected in the eternal scheme of things, we bow before you today in thanksgiving for love and life and all the kinds of energy that constitute our existence. It is by your grace that we live and move and have our being. It is by your will that we become aware of relationships and patterns and surprises that make our lives meaningful. Help us to be more fully yours, that we may be more completely open and receptive to all your gifts. Make us aware of all we have to give to the world around us: care and compassion, words and deeds of encouragement, assistance in food and money and clothing and medicine and shelter, and, above all, the hope of the gospel, that all peoples are one in Christ Jesus, and heirs of your love and kingdom. Forgive us for times of selfish concern in our lives—for worrying about *our* health and *our* income and *our* happiness and *our* slice of the pie. Then we shall praise you with real praise, and make a joyful noise among all the peoples of the world to the God of our mutual salvation. To that end, O God, hear our prayers and give strength to the intentions of our hearts, through Jesus Christ our Lord and Master. Amen.

20

O God, who has called and ordained us to be a special people in the world, we thank you for the church and its ministries. We are grateful for this community of faith in which we are challenged to grow and to become more conformed to the image of Jesus Christ. As Jesus loved the church and gave himself for it, help us to make our own commitments to it, thereby strengthening both the church and ourselves. Bless, we pray, all the saints who are troubled this day by ill health or confused minds or broken relationships or financial need. Send your Spirit upon those who are having difficulty feeling your presence. Transform those who seek the wrong things in life, and minister to those who seek the right things, but seem to have little success in finding them. Inspire us all to love mercy, to act justly, and to live in humility with you. Let us use whatever we have to share with others in their needs, and to bind up the wounds of a world forever at war. Grant us strength to walk from day to day, and faith to see beyond the present age to the time when all nations will be gathered up in you, when swords will be beaten into plowshares, when the lion will lie down with the lamb and the bear will eat straw with the ox. Through Jesus Christ our Lord. Amen.

21

A Pastoral Prayer for Young People

O God, we pray this morning for all our young people. This is a hard time in which to be growing up, with many pressures and lots of confusion. They receive conflicting messages from their parents, who say "Be this way" and then live another way. They are lured by television and the movies to desire a life of glamor and wealth and easy sex, and, when they reach for these things, find in them apples of dust and vials of poison. They are goaded by friends and acquaintances to drink and take drugs and have sex, and then discover that their friends were not friends at all. They long for a world that is beautiful and fruitful and peaceful, but are reminded every day that our planet could be incinerated in a matter of hours. What hope is there for them, dear God, except the hope you have given us in Christ Jesus our Lord? Lift their eyes to a cross far away, and to the man who died on it, his heart peaceful, his soul composed because his trust was in you. Help them to cast their cares upon him, to pledge their lives to him, to follow him with all their gifts and energies. Let them hear him call their names—Mark, Sue, Ernesto, Amelia—and walk after him as boys and girls who have fallen in love with God. Save them from the perilous times in which we exist. Teach them to live in such a way that their time will not be wasted on this earth. Help them to renounce self and selfish pleasure to become servants of the world. Pour your power and patience and love on all who attempt to lead the young, and on all parents, that the example set before their children may be the example of Christ living in our midst. Give us the grace to put our arms around one another, young and old alike, and to say "I love you, how can I help you?" and to discover in the mutuality of our compassion something about the kingdom of God. In the name of Jesus, who grew to manhood in the world without losing his sense of eternity. Amen.

22

O God, who transcends the small worries and anxieties of our lives, help us to transcend them too. Let us find such peace and joy in you that everything else in life assumes its proper perspective. Teach us to be less concerned about ourselves and more caring about your world. Show us how to find pleasure in giving ourselves to others, in small ways and large. Help us to develop sensitivities to their feelings, and to know how to put our arms around them when they hurt. Give comfort especially to those who are walking in grief, remembering a loved one whose steps are no longer heard and whose touch is no longer there. Let us live so constantly in the spirit and mood of prayer that Christ becomes all in all and there is no longer a clear line of definition between this world and the next. Lead us to invest our treasures in your kingdom, that our hearts may be there, too. Befriend the young, who are often rebellious and alone. Instruct the parents, who are sometimes confused and weary. Strengthen the aged, who find things more difficult than they once did. Aid the jobless and the poor, that they may be led to greener pastures. Rescue the drug addict and the alcoholic, and return them to the joy of self-control. Guide all who are lost and wandering in the maze of life's choices. And enfold us at last in your arms, that, having enjoyed the world of your creation, we may finally rest in the bosom of the Creator, through Jesus Christ our Lord. Amen.

23

Spirit of the living God, fall fresh on us. Let the peace and stillness of your eternal kingdom, so different from the warring madness of the world, enable us to feel a deep sense of worship. Speak to our hearts of the things that matter most: of eternal unity with Christ; of loving relationships with family and friends; of caring for the good earth; of living creatively, sensitively, and joyfully. Help us to commit ourselves to causes that are substantial and everlasting, and that will be productive for all generations. Save us from boastfulness, from wrong behavior, and from false allegiances. Restore those who grieve and those who suffer from illness, rejection, or brokenness of any kind. Reveal to us and in us your plan for the nations of the world. As the gentle streams find their beginning in the hills and then flow down to water the earth, let us discover our strength in you and then go out to bless the people and institutions beyond these walls. Lead us to be more than a self-centered fellowship dwelling upon our own problems and desires; make us into the Church of Jesus the Redeemer, that loses itself in obedience to your heavenly will. Let the power that was upon your Son be given through us to all peoples, that your name may be glorified in all the earth. For yours are the power and the glory forever and ever. Amen.

24

Lord, teach us to pray. Help us to come before you in quietness and sincerity, and, shutting out the world around us, become so immersed in your spirit that you are for us the supreme reality. Let us lay hold of the power that moves mountains and casts them into the sea, or, more important, let that power lay hold of us, that our lives may be completely surrendered. Then show us how to put our arms around the poor and hungry of the world, and to plead their case before you until the very doors of heaven must open to their poverty and neglect. Teach us how to seek healing for those ravaged by disease or loss of health, those afflicted by nervous or chemical disorders, those troubled in mind and spirit. Help us to know how to pray for our leaders, and all who make far-reaching decisions in the social and political world, that they may be wholesome and godly in their spirits, wise in their thinking, and com- passionate in their discharge of duty. Enable us to be mind- ful of the millions of people who live as prisoners or refugees or street-dwellers, without any chance at the ordi- nary life we take for granted. Instruct us in praying for alcoholics and drug addicts, for criminals and terrorists, for pimps and prostitutes and pornographers. Aid us in sup- porting with our prayers the teachers, ministers, mission- aries, social workers, legal assistants, and others who envision a better world for all and labor to give it birth. Direct us in praying for peace and justice among the nations, that we may care more for your kingdom than for our own status or welfare. Let your spirit, that was in Christ Jesus our Lord, be in us, forming us to pray and offering in us the prayers that are acceptable to you, O God, our hope and our redeemer, to whom be glory forever and ever. Amen.

25

O God, who changes rivers in their courses and alters the paths of the stars, come now and direct us into new ways of thinking and living that will bring us to perfect joy in you. Help us to be willing to risk everything in pursuit of your kingdom. Speak winningly to those whose minds are tired or bored or committed to routine. Rekindle happiness in those whose hearts have been bowed down in grief. Put sparkle in the eyes of those who felt defeated or broken. Set the cross once more in our midst and remind us of the life that springs out of death and the hope that rises from despair. Let all our problems and illnesses be but the turn- ing in the road that brings us back to you, and then bestow new energy, new understanding, new imagination upon us. We commit to your care our children, that they may know you; our elderly, that they may rejoice in you; our friends and loved ones who are ill, that they may trust in you; the leaders of our world, that they may bow down to you; and our church, that it may serve you. Through Jesus Christ our Savior. Amen.

26

O God, whose righteousness is as burning as the sun, yet whose mercy covers all things as the night, we confess to you the inadequacy of our souls to come into your presence. We have not drawn aside from the course of life to pray and meditate as we ought, nor have we attended to others with that constant love and concern recommended by Christ. We have been too anxious about ourselves and our own affairs, and have not worshiped you with our whole hearts. Forgive us, we pray, and renew us by your Spirit. Teach us to awaken in the morning with joy and to live through the day with sensitivity and gratitude. Bring to flower in us the gifts of kindness and generosity. Let the peace and fullness that are in you flow out through us to our friends and loved ones, and to this community, and to the whole world. Make us vassals of your Christ and vessels of your grace. Touch our sick with healing and our broken ones with wholeness. Guard our young people from throwing away their inheritance before they know its value. Strengthen our families. Support those who live alone. Grant to this congregation the will and the wisdom to become your church, preferring your presence above all riches and supporting the poor and the outcast and seeking your way beyond all our personal desires. For yours are the power and the glory forever. Amen.

27

In the heat and stillness of a summer morning, O God, we rest ourselves in your presence. Some of us have carried heavy loads this week. Some have been troubled about health problems, in ourselves or in loved ones. Some have worried about finances, and how to make things work in an expensive and difficult world. Others have been upset about human relationships: about parents or children who don't understand, spouses who no longer care, friends who have given little support. Still others have been worried about the great metaphysical problems of life: What is it all about? What does it mean? Why is there suffering? Is there life after death? If God is real, why does God permit the existence of so much injustice and unhappiness in the world? We know you are real, O God. Here in this place the air is thick with your presence. The faith of our fathers and mothers, and their fathers and mothers before them, assures us not only of your existence but of your love and care for us. Confident of this, O God, let us relax and leave our heavy loads with you, who are able to bear them with so much more strength. Teach us to turn from anxiety to thanksgiving, and to let our hearts leap up with lightness and joy at the sound of your name. Show us how to find excitement in one another, refreshment in our opportunities for service, and direction in the needs of our world. And let all the great questions of life find their solution for us in the death of Christ on Calvary and in his Resurrection from the grave. For yours is the mystery and the glory forever and ever. Amen.

28

A Pastoral Prayer for Graduation Sunday

God of the ages, we especially hold before you today these young men and women who have completed their high school education and stand at one of the great crossroads of life. We are grateful for their time among us as members of our families and our church. Now we commit them to you for the significant time and experiences that lie ahead of them. Grant them a sense of your presence wherever their journeys lead, to watch over them, protect them, and direct them in paths of righteousness and fulfillment. Anoint them with love and insight, that they may be open to wholesome relationships and opportunities for growth. Teach them gentleness and humility, that they may not be at war within themselves or with others. But grant them also a sense of firmness and justice, that they may defend truth and goodness wherever they go. Send special grace on their families, who in many cases must now give them up to make their way in the world. Let their grief at parting be turned to joy in new experiences with the family members who remain, or with friends and associates who are also deserving of love and relationship. Let your Spirit rest today upon all our young people, including those who study or work or live away from us. Shelter them beneath your everlasting wings, as the hen shelters her brood, and lead them always into relationships and situations that will reward their souls. Grant to the new generation a care for things eternal, and the knowledge to bring peace and justice to the world in a way their parents failed to do. Let your kingdom come in their hearts, and in ours as well, and we shall give you the glory and praise forever and ever. Amen.

29

O God, whose holiness is like the clouds of the heavens, we bow before you, expectant of rain. Apart from you, our lives become arid and useless. Turned in upon ourselves, we become vain and anxious, weak and troubled; our hearts commit mistakes and our appetites incline us to pleasures that add little to our well-being. Shower your love and spirit upon us, that our souls may slake their thirst in you and the things that are in heaven, and that we may more sensitively adore the world you have given us. Teach us to love you by loving the prisoner, the person on food stamps, the clerk who was unkind to us, the hostile friend, the clever enemy. Show us the way of peace, which will come to earth only when all people share the little they have to make a feast of plenty. Help us to be militant for the things that matter in life, and friendly and indifferent about the things that don't. Give us energy for caring, for reaching out to others, for improving government, for planting flowers along life's way, and make us tired of protecting our turf, projecting false images of ourselves, stockpiling money and goods we don't need, and preparing for war. Let Christ, who was simple and good and direct, walk among us now, touching the sick, lifting up the fallen, redirecting the confused, and calling us all to follow him. For yours (and his) is the kingdom that lasts forever, and must overcome the kingdoms of this world. Amen.

30

We come to you, O God, at a time when much of our nation has been gripped by snow and cold, when roads have been clogged and winds have been bitter and many people have been forced into public shelters to keep warm. Let the metaphor of coldness raise the question of our own spiritual temperatures. Has our relationship to you been frozen and stiff? Are the ways of our hearts clogged by snowdrifts of apathy and indifference? Do the lines of communication between us sag and break beneath the iciness of neglect or rebellion? Forgive us, O God, and send a warming trend into our lives. Let there be a melting of our hearts and a surrender to your will and your way. Grant that the icicles of pride and refusal may fall from our personalities, and that the heat of your love and grace may break up the ice floes that have kept us apart. Transform us into centers of warmth and growth that will radiate your presence into the coldhearted world around us. Give healing to our sick and hope to those who are depressed. Let the truly humble discover a sense of self-esteem. Grant peace to those who are anxious and renewal to those who are tired. Cure us of lust and greed and boredom by sending Christ to stand in our midst. In fact, O God, let him but come and touch us now and all our problems shall be small ones, dwarfed in the magnitude and beauty of his presence. In him there is never coldness, but eternal springtime and the dancing of fountains. Come, Lord Jesus, and help us to worship with warmth and passion, for your name's sake. Amen.

31

O God, who watches over us even when we make our journeys into far countries of the spirit and waste our inheritance in self-indulgent ways, we give thanks for your patience and faithfulness and love. Help us to come to ourselves in this time of worship, and see what our lives are really like in the eternal scheme of things. We are so prone to follow our own paths and to miss the path of goodness and righteousness. We seize momentary pleasures instead of striving for everlasting goals. We gratify our selfish desires instead of seeking the welfare of others. Enable us in this hour to choose another way, that will lead us home to you, where life is sound and loving and generous. Let these hearts of stone and indifference become hearts of tenderness and sensitivity. And as we experience your forgiving arms around us, let our whole outlook on life become new, filled with joy and excitement and enthusiasm, as it was when we were children. For we are indeed your children, O God, humbled and chastened by what we have seen of life, and hungry to set our feet beneath your heavenly table once more and share in the life of the family that bears your name, through Jesus Christ our Lord. Amen.

32

Many of us, O God, are insurance-poor—we carry car insurance, house insurance, health insurance, accident insurance, life insurance, disaster insurance, work insurance, retirement insurance, travel insurance, package insurance, luggage insurance, moving insurance, professional insurance, educational insurance, liability insurance—and our *souls* are perishing for lack of attention. Teach us how to care for the things that are most valuable: the minds and hearts of those around us, the good earth you have given us, our relationship to you. Give us the spirit of prayer, that we may live in communion with you. Let holiness and not ownership be our goal in life. Show us your will and let us follow it, becoming missionaries of love and renewal and wholeness in our community and the world around us. Heal the dividedness and brokenness in our personalities. Take away our anger and resentment. Make us feel good about life, and therefore about ourselves. Lead us into gentleness and contemplation and faithfulness and generosity. Reveal through us your power to change lives and redeem the human situation. And let us learn to praise you as the giver of all mercy, O Lord, our strength and our salvation. Amen.

33

A Pastoral Prayer for Mother's Day

O God, whom our Lord Jesus called "Father" because that was the symbol of power and lineage and protection in his day, but whom we know increasingly today as "Mother" because you are also nurturing and birth-giving and care-taking, we come into your presence as children, laying aside our cares and responsibilities to enjoy you and worship you and be renewed in your presence. Help us to discover here our true natures and to realign the inner and outer aspects of our existence. Teach us to live by faith, and thus to be at peace in our souls. Show us how to keep the part of us that matters most from being bartered away in the marketplace or lost in the shuffle of schedules and agendas. Grant that the love you have always shown your people, and want to show us, will keep us from anxiety and from spending our energies in ways that do not contribute to your kingdom or to our happiness. Today we remember and give thanks for our mothers—for the hopes and dreams of their lives, for the love with which they carried us in their wombs, for the hours they expended in bathing and feeding and teaching us, for the tenderness and companionship that were often the bonuses of our relationships with them. We pray for all mothers here, and ask for them continued strength to love and care for the world. We remember those especially who have lost children and suffer an emptiness because they can no longer touch or fondle the flesh of their flesh. Grant to all of us the hope of eternal life, whereby we believe that no special relationship will ever be lost, but that all will be gathered forever in your perfect love and kept by the grace of your Holy Spirit. Give abundantly of yourself now to all who are gathered here, particularly those who come with troubled hearts or physical needs of any kind. Let the love that is your transcendent nature be our nature too, that we may share with one another joy and warmth and genuine caring, and go from this place with the bread of heaven to give to all who ask, in the name of Jesus Christ our Savior. Amen.

34
A Pastoral Prayer for Father's Day

O God, who was so protective and loving and creative that Jesus called you Father, we offer our prayer today for the fathers of the world. Help them not to be so busy that they miss their children's childhoods. Teach them to love, and to care about feelings and little things, that the whole world may be richer. Let them be gentle and loving to their children's mothers, in order that families may be strong and joyous. Show them how to relax and to play, and not to be so worried and caught up in things that don't matter. Grant that they may have faithful relationships to you, that they may be models of honesty and spirituality and wholesome love to their children. And give us all a tender respect for fatherhood, so that we may live in natural order with your creation. Remind us today of the fathers of our faith, who braved the seas, crossed mountains, fought with wild beasts, and died in prisons in order to keep alive the gospel of our Lord Jesus. Deepen our commitment to what they believed in, and increase our strength for meeting the demands of the gospel in a complex world. Comfort the sad and lonely, give heart to the discouraged, heal the sick, save the young, and reveal yourself to us in the word that is spoken today by your servant, for we pray in the name of Christ Jesus our Lord. Amen.

35

A Pastoral Prayer for Independence Day

On the eve of our nation's birthday, O God, we praise you for its star-spangled history: for patriots' dreams and purple mountains' majesties, for soldiers' deaths and farmers' fields, for rivers and plains and refineries and factories, for schools and churches and assembly halls, for scientists and statesmen and coal miners and teachers, for truck drivers and lawyers, for astronauts and cartoonists and engineers and secretaries. It is an illustrious, staggering panorama, and we are proud of the red, white, and blue. But O God, there is no god like you. Whatever is good and wonderful and beautiful about our country is a gift from you; and whatever is wrong with it, alien to its grand dreams and hopes—the greed, the injustice, the crime, the arrogance, the profiteering—is due to our own failure of purpose and commitment. Give us the spirit to love our country and yet to be critical; help us always to love your kingdom more. We hold up to you our president and his cabinet; the Congress and Supreme Court; the governors and legislatures of our states; the mayors and councils of our cities. Crown them, dear God, with vision, honesty, and compassion. Let each of them worship you today and be a more committed leader tomorrow. Redeem us from our sinful ways. Restore us to our rightful minds. And let the flag that has flown over our country all these years fly yet with honor and purpose, for yours is the kingdom and the power and the glory forever. Amen.

36

O God, who created us of the earth and yet made us for eternity, so that we are always unhappy with ourselves until we have found peace in you, we open our lives to you now for your blessings. Receive us in our pain and brokenness, and let us be healed through seeing the unity of all that you have made. Restore to us the vision of a world where the poor are loved and the outcasts are given a home. Teach us to walk in true humility of spirit, that everything around us may be open and hospitable to us. Ensure in us the meaning of the gospel, that your kingdom may come in our midst. Lay your gentle hands upon the sick of our community, that they may be healed, and upon those who mourn the loss of loved ones, that they may be comforted. Guard the hearts and minds of our children, that they may be kept from waste and evil. Anoint the souls of the aged, that they may be prepared for the life to come. Touch the altars of your church with fire, that the offerings of self and goods may be consumed in holiness, for your name's sake. And grant that our worship in this hour may be acceptable in your sight, O Lord, our strength and our redeemer. Amen.

37

O God, it is a dangerous thing we are about to ask, and we know it. But we pray that we may have the consciousness of Christ in our lives. We would like to be aware of you as he was aware of you: to know your naked heart of love, to know the glory of your righteousness, to know your infinite concern about the imbalances and injustices of life. We would like to see the world as he saw it: teeming with people who need healing and care and compassion. We would like to share in his vision of the kingdom: of the way it reorders people's lives and reorganizes priorities and either redeems or destroys human institutions. But we know this is dangerous. For to pray this way is to invite upon ourselves the possibilities given shape in Jesus himself: of being called to specific forms of ministry, of being thought brash or blasphemous or even crazy, of being despised as troublemakers, of being nailed to a cross. Creating a world isn't easy, is it, God? It is a long, hard, suffering business. You have suffered over it for centuries. Give us, we pray, the courage and resolution to join you, and, not counting the cost, become cocreators with you. Let the desires that were in Christ Jesus be in us also, that, being united to him, we shall reveal to the world around us the dream you have for your creation, that we all may be one, sharing life and love and possessions, until we are caught up in the heavenly kingdom. For yours are the kingdom and the power and the glory forever. Amen.

38

A Pastoral Prayer for Memorial Day, All Saints, or Anniversary Sunday

God of the ages, who was old when the world was born and are young now that it is old, we lift our hearts on this day of remembrance to praise you for all your acts of kindness and for all the saints who have stood in the faith before us. We thank you for the steadfast hope of the patriarchs and the prophets, for the blessed ministry and death and Resurrection of our Lord, and for the endurance of the Apostles through every trial and tribulation. We acknowledge the long line of priests and believers through the centuries, and all of those who taught us the gospel in our own generation. Especially do we remember those who were most dear to us—fathers and mothers, brothers and sisters, and even children—who have been gathered up to life everlasting while we continue our pilgrimages here. Give us strength, O God, to maintain the journeys they have begun, looking always to Jesus, the author and perfecter of our faith. Teach us to share what we have with the world, and so enrich all people as we travel. Remove from us all selfishness and fear and lack of faith, and enable us to love with openness and courage. Strengthen your church through our service, and bring us all at last into the kingdom of heaven, where we shall continue to remember and praise you, world without end. Amen.

39

Lord, we thank you for days when nothing goes wrong: when the dishwasher works and the computer doesn't get our charge account fouled up and the mail doesn't bring any bad news and the car doesn't overheat the way it sometimes does and little Suzie doesn't fall out of the swing and break her arm and Mama's arthritis doesn't act up and the dog doesn't get trash all over the yard and the rain doesn't come in and flood the basement. These are the days that enable us to get by, to absorb the strength and relaxation to deal with the other days. Sometimes we forget to be grateful for them, even though we never fail to call on you when things are going badly. So thank you, Lord, for all the good days. They really help. Amen.

40

The world is gift, O God, and we thank you for it—for earth to till and sky to mount, for flowers to smell and trees to climb, for friends to cheer and loved ones to embrace. Forgive us for days when we do not see the beauty of it all—when we are distracted by ambition or work or a selfish nature. Mold us more in the image of Christ, who never lost sight of the gift. Let his care for the disciples lead us to deeper relationships with friends. Let his gentleness with children give us a higher regard for play and fantasy. Let his courage before the cross imbue us with strength for the trials of life. Let his Resurrection instill in us new confidence in the life to come, taking away our fear and tension. Your grace is measureless, O God; help us to soar in it, and not remain so earthbound. For yours is the kingdom and the power and the glory forever and ever. Amen.

41

O God, who broods over us at night like a mother bird over her nest and rises upon us in the morning like the sun that warms the earth, we lift our hearts to you in worship and adoration, praising you for the gift of life and the sense of your presence. Contritely, we ask for the forgiveness of our sins, and for the assuaging of all hate and envy and bitterness from our lives. Let the radiant power of your Holy Spirit destroy the negativity in us and fill us with positive feelings of love and affirmation. Help us to say yes to the things that are good and beautiful today, and no to the things that hinder or devalue life. Enable us to reach out to one another as brothers and sisters in Christ, confessing our faults, embracing those we thought were enemies, and discovering the joy of all our relationships in you. Heal our minds and our hearts and our bodies. And grant that we, as the people of God, may go out from here today with healing for the broken, despondent peoples of the world, whether in the ghettos or country clubs of this city, or in the stone and bamboo huts of other nations. Let the gifts you have entrusted to us, of money and ingenuity and technical skill, become the means by which the good news of your kingdom and your loving care reaches to the uttermost parts of the earth. Through him whose name we praise for having brought us this news through his own death on the cross and Resurrection from the grave, even Jesus Christ our Lord. Amen.

42

O God, who is seen in the gold and crimson landscape of autumn, in the blue skies and stubbly fields of corn and pyramids of orange and yellow pumpkins, we remember that you are also seen in the faces of starving children and the crusty hands of farmers; the wrinkled bodies of the old and the vacant eyes of prisoners; in the downcast looks of the grieving and the willing attitudes of nurses, teachers, social workers, and others who are trying to make the world a better and easier place in which to live. Give us eyes to see you at work, and hearts that are sensitive to your presence. Help us to be better conduits of your grace, that the few loaves and fishes passing through our hands may feed the multitudes who need them. Comfort the lonely and give strength to those who struggle with personal problems. Endue the various committees and individuals of this congregation with wisdom and power to accomplish their several duties, and let your church be a community of love and healing for all whose lives are within its reach. Bless your Word wherever it goes forth in the world today, and let your people praise your name with joy and thanksgiving for their constant renewal and heavenly fellowship. For yours are the kingdom and the glory forever. Amen.

43

A Pastoral Prayer for Thanksgiving

O God of song and saga, of earth and history, we thank you for the rich heritage of our nation: for pilgrim's feet and patriot's dream; for "fruited plain" and "purple mountain majesties"; for factories and commerce and universities and churches; for Indian and Irish and Chinese and Puerto Rican and Kenyan and Greek; for Protestant and Catholic and Jew, and Mormon, Amish, and Muslim. We pray for the dedication to preserve and further enrich this noble environment: to keep alive the dream; to cleanse the streams and the air and the land; to protect the forests and rebuild the roads; to reconsecrate the cities and the hopes of those who live in them; to humanize industry and make humanity more godlike; to develop the sciences for the good of humanity, and to further the arts for the delight and profit of our species; to deepen the sense of communication among races and individuals; and to increase the tolerance for diversity, and promote goodwill among those of differing backgrounds and experiences. Keep us from the fear that divides and the cynicism that corrupts, and let the Spirit that was in Christ Jesus our Lord unite our hearts and minds for the future welfare of this land, that we may praise you forever as one nation under God. Amen.

44

A Pastoral Prayer for Thanksgiving

O God of summer and winter, heat and cold, dark and light, we thank you for the varieties of life we meet in you: for the delight of quiet and lonely moments, and for the joy of families reunited; for the taste of afternoon tea and the sumptuousness of a Thanksgiving feast; for the sound of a fly buzzing on a windowsill and the amplitude of a magnificent choir singing in the sanctuary; for the smile of a walker passed in the street and the wraparound warmth of a congregation gathered in the name of Christ. The world is a theater of your glory, and a gallery of your loving care. Help us to see it, O God. Remove the blinders of jealousy and ambition and self-preoccupation that cheat us of an unrestricted view. Immerse us in your spirit, that we may live in the world as those who enjoy it and not as those who try to own it. Endue us with loving attitudes, that we may walk humbly in the canyons of commerce, in the halls of intellect, and in the corridors of service. Let the presence of Christ, crucified and risen, be upon us all, healing our brokenness, mending our resolve, and uniting us in the kingdom now and forever. Amen.

45

A Pastoral Prayer for Advent

Come, Lord Jesus, into a world that is twisted and broken by sin, that lives in fear and hate and self-despising. Come with your strength and honesty, your purity and power, and teach us to follow you. Give courage and vision to our leaders, that they may show us peace and not war, freedom and not burdens. Inspire a new generation of young people to be clean and moral and hopeful, that they may be strong leaders for tomorrow. Show us how to prefer gentleness to brutality, and civility to outrage. Let us speak once more of faith, hope, and love, and follow the paths that lead to life everlasting instead of pleasure for the moment. Come, Lord Jesus, and renew your spirit in each of us as we wait before you. Scatter our sin as the sun scatters the night. Lift our hearts at the sound of your voice, make us to bow down at the rustle of your garments. Let illness flee and selfishness depart. Give wholeness and joy and a desire to love our brothers and sisters. Come, Lord Jesus, and let the truth of your incarnation fill our souls and minds once more. Banish illusion and unveil reality to our tired lives.

Let us see you in your glory, you who were born in a stable bare and crucified on a tree. Open our eyes to angels, our ears to hymns of praise; and make this Christmas the best one ever, as more needed by our world. Come, Lord Jesus, for we are your people and we wait for you now, for your name's sake. Amen.

46

A Pastoral Prayer for Advent

In the hurry and worry of getting ready for Christmas, O Lord, help us to be quiet and not miss the real beauty and truth of the season. Let the glory that shone on the shepherds on the hillside shine on us, illuminating our lives with peace and joy. Enable us to see beyond the commonplace and be in touch with the eternal that has visited us in Christ. Grant healing to all who are sick and afflicted, and contentment to all who are troubled. Give comfort to all who are separated from loved ones, either by distance or by death or by dissension. Show us how to live at peace within ourselves and with others. Reveal yourself to the poor and homeless of this area, that they may live in hope of a better life to come. Grant that those of us who can read and live in good homes and have plenty of food may learn to share with others, that they may have what is rightfully theirs, and that we may become true citizens of your kingdom. Now teach us to listen to the wild, irrational voices in our hearts and abandon ourselves to higher ways than the ones we have followed. Let Christ enter this building, even as he entered the stable of Bethlehem, and shed his glorious illumination on us, that we may be changed and follow him forever; for there is nothing here as rich as what he brought to the stable. Amen.

47
A Pastoral Prayer for Christmas

Those who waited in darkness, O God, have seen a great light, and on them has the light shone brightly. Send the light again, dear God, to shine in our darkness—the darkness of doubt, the darkness of sin, the darkness of loneliness, the darkness of fear and confusion. Let the presence of the One laid in a manger illumine our hearts and minds, that our whole lives may be transformed. May the simplicity of his entrance into the world call us again to the simple way of living. May the coming of the shepherds remind us that there is more to do in life than tend our flocks or supervise our businesses. May the adoration of the Magi teach us that we too have gifts to bring. May the joy of aged Anna and Simeon suggest patterns for our own aging and its relationship to your eternal kingdom. And as the Christmas bells ring out once more across the land, publishing good tidings of great joy, let our small hearts respond with excitement and love, that the light has shone in darkness and the darkness has not overcome it, even in our own time. Amen.

48
A Pastoral Prayer for Christmas

O God, who is known in the bleakness of wilderness as well as in the magic of this Christmas season, who abides with your children in times of suffering and hardship as well as in times of joy and plenty, hear now the prayers we make from our various places in life. Give peace and strength to those who are lonely or distressed or angry. Grant rest and renewal to those who are tired. Touch with healing all bodies that are sick, minds that are disturbed, hearts that ache. Make whole the relationships that have been broken, and give new relationships where life is barren and sterile. Create your beautiful kingdom inside us, and help us to share it with others. Bring us to a right consideration of the things in our lives, that we may not seek them or grasp them, but use them for the needs of the poor and hungry. Teach us to be imaginative with all our gifts, that they may bless the world, and, blessing the world, bless us as well. Anoint our children with a sense of wonder and reverence that will never leave them, and enable those of us who are older to rediscover a feeling for mystery during this special season of the year. Make us aware of your presence in little things—a cup of tea, a flickering candle, a gentle smile—that we may seek life and not death, love and not self-destruction. Through him who was born at Bethlehem in order that we might live forever. Amen.

49
A Pastoral Prayer for Christmas

We live in the real world, O God, of pain and hunger and crime and violence and drugs and death. Help us to remember that Christmas is about the real world too: the pain of childbearing, the humility of birth, the anger and violence of those who are threatened, the poor who are always clamoring for bread, the sick always waiting to be healed, the dying and their families who cry out of their impotence for some eternal hand to save them. Let this season of the year be a time of deep spiritual renewal for all of us. Give us the kingdom and help us to know what it means that it has come. Let the baby who was born at Bethlehem reign in our hearts. Turn the tragedy of the world into the triumph of your grace. Let all who are sick or tired or bereaved or encumbered with guilt see the star shining brightly over the manger and lead them there. Teach us to kneel down, and kneeling, to find joy and peace for our souls. Transform our vision, that we may see the world differently. Let us see it as you see it. Help us to see the hungry of the world waiting on us for bread. Help us to see the sick waiting to be touched and comforted. Help us to see the lonely waiting to be embraced. Help us to see the angry waiting to be loved. Give us your mystical presence, O God. Let our communion extend beyond the hymns and prayers and words that are spoken here. Be real in our midst. Make us the Church. For Christmas is coming, and we seek a miracle. Through Jesus Christ our Lord. Amen.

50

A Pastoral Prayer for Christmas

Our hearts beat faster and our adrenaline flows more heavily at this time of the year, O God. We respond to the lights and decorations, to the glad sounds of music, to the prospects of gifts and brightly decked houses and parties and friends and relatives coming to call. But help us not to forget, O Holy One of Israel, that the origin of all joy is in your love and self-giving, which were made known most completely in the child born at Bethlehem. Teach us to be still and to touch the joy. Let it flow through us like some eternal medicine, healing our hurts and wounds and illnesses. Let it perfume the air we breathe, filling us with its sweetness. Let it ring through the corridors of our minds like heavenly bells, tolling happiness and fellowship and a peace we have never really known. And when we have felt it, when it has flowed through us and perfumed the air around us and rung in our minds like the pealing of bells, let it move out from us to everyone we meet and know. Let the true spirit of Christmas begin in us and gradually take over the world, converting hate to love, greed to generosity, and ignorance to enlightenment. Grant mercy to the self-driven. Open the arms of the shy and retiring. Give blessedness to the broken in heart. And let the song of the angels be our song, as we are drawn together in the name of him who was born and died in Judea to save the world from its sin. Amen.

51
A Pastoral Prayer for Children at Christmas

O God, who has spoken to us through a baby born in Bethlehem, we pray this morning for the children of the world and their future. We ask for them the kind of society where children are valued and loved for who they are, not for what they can mean to a government or an army or an economy; where parents are encouraged to place their children's welfare above wages and extra income; where teachers of the young are treasured above industrialists and generals and financiers; where parks and playgrounds are given a higher priority than missiles and aircraft carriers. Bless, we pray, all who minister to children: the doctors and nurses and therapists who devote themselves to infants' birth and health; the social workers who agonize over slum conditions and unhappy homes; the teachers and coaches and counselors who labor tirelessly to train their minds and bodies and perceptions; the institutional helpers who dedicate their lives to caring for special children; and all the parents and aunts and uncles and grandparents and friends who love them and surround their lives with the grace to grow and experience the world in warm and pleasant ways. Help us all to be more sensitive to the feelings of children— to their longings and desires, their loneliness and their love—and to act upon that sensitivity with the kind of thoughtfulness and generosity that will make us more childlike. And now we commit to you all children in this sanctuary, that their lives may be shaped in a Christlike atmosphere, and that together we may worship you in the beauty of holiness, O God of the Christmas story. Amen.

52

A Pastoral Prayer for Christmas Eve

O Lord of Christmas, whose breath is mercy and whose arms are grace, we crowd before you as the lost, the tired, the confused, and the amazed. Still the fluttering of our hearts with your divine calmness, and touch our eyes until they see your advent here. Teach us to be simple and good in our lives, affecting only those things that make for love and joy and peace among us. Help us to share our bread with the hungry of the world and our hearts with the lonely. Let the glitter of tinsel and the light from our candles be dim beside the glow of our happiness in Christ. Draw us once more on that ancient pilgrimage to Bethlehem and permit us to stand in awe before the sight that made angels sing and kings produce their treasures. Grant that the peace that passes all human understanding may settle upon the nations of the world, until shepherds watching their flocks by night are more important than satellites watching Washington and Moscow and Beijing. Turn us into the way of the Messiah, that we may prefer justice and love to power and wealth. Show us the beauty of a star and the innocence of a maid and the simplicity of a stable and the glory of a Child, that we may be reclaimed from all our errant ways and reborn in the spirit of Christmas. For your name's sake. Amen.

53

A Pastoral Prayer for the Sunday After Christmas

On this Sunday after Christmas, Lord, many of us are like the son in Jesus' story who went and spent all, and, finding himself in want, returned to the father's house. Some of us have spent all our money—even money we didn't have. Bless us for our generosity and good intentions. Some of us have spent all our energy. Give us rest and peace and refreshment of soul. And some of us, more seriously, have spent our faith and our capacity to share in the fellowship and dreams of the human community. As the year draws to a close, help us to remember with thankfulness the good moments it has held, and to lay to rest without fear or guilt the bad ones. Usher us into a new year with the will to find new insights and live with new strength. You are the living water; teach us to drink daily from your well. You are the bread of life; teach us to eat daily until we are filled. Give peace to the troubled, wholeness to the sick, companionship to the lonely, resourcefulness to the shallow, commitment to the fainthearted, and joy to the broken in spirit. Let the months before us bring rest to a weary world and hope to millions who dwell in darkness. And use us who wait before you to accomplish your will, through devotion and imagination and love. In Jesus' name. Amen.

54
A Pastoral Prayer for New Year Sunday

God of all beginnings, and God of all middles and endings as well, we bow in your presence at the start of this new year to confess our dependence on you. Everything good that has ever happened to us, all the good fortune of our days, we owe to you. Without you, we would have been overwhelmed by our difficulties, by all the natural disasters to which our flesh is prone. Only by your grace through Jesus Christ do we understand life as we do, and value those things that give structure and meaning to our existence. Therefore we pray for your guidance and help in the year to come. We know that the way to life and blessedness is narrow, and that few there are who truly find it. Be our guide, O Lord, through the temptations and trials of another year. Help us to choose wisely in all our decisions. Enable us to do justice, to love mercy, and to walk humbly before you. Show us how to love you with all our hearts, and our neighbors as ourselves. Make us doers of the word and not hearers only. Let us learn to take up our crosses and follow him who died on Calvary for the sins of the world. Teach us not to worry about what the other disciple is doing, but to be faithful about what we have been given to do. Lead us beyond standing about, gazing up into heaven, that we may preach the gospel to all who need it, baptizing and teaching them in the name of your Son. And grant that when the new year is ended we may hear you say, "Well done, good and faithful servant." Through Jesus Christ our Lord. Amen.

55
A Pastoral Prayer for New Year Sunday

Most merciful God, whose love is as constant as the shining of the sun beyond the clouds and whose ways are deeper than any ocean depths, we bow before you at the beginning of a new year to ask that it may be a year lived in your will and your grace. Let your Spirit come freshly upon us, that we may be different in the days ahead. Teach us humility, that we shall not act in our own conceit. Give us love for every creature and every creation, that we may walk reverently in the world. Instill in us a sense of wonder, that we may see your presence everywhere. Impart to the worried new confidence, and to the fearful a sense of trust. Raise up the sick and distraught with an impulse to praise. Comfort the mournful heart and reveal fellowship to the lonely. Quicken our sensibilities, deepen our compassion, and stir up our commitment, that we may live this day and through the year as children of the covenant, created, called out, and commissioned by him whose name is above every name, even Jesus our Lord. Amen.

56

O God, who created the heavens and the earth, the moon and the stars, the mountains and the valleys and the seas, we are creators too: we have created poverty and pollution and starvation, crime and squalor and injustice; we have made fear and prejudice and enmity, and greed and dishonesty and war. Forgive us, we pray, as we enter another year. Restore to us hope and trust and compassion. Let mercy run down like the mountain streams, and grace like a waterfall. Teach us to walk again in belief, honesty, and commitment. Let the sanity of your divine presence overcome the madness and horror of living in the world we have made, that Christ may be exalted and your name glorified, both now and in all time to come. Amen.

57

In the aura of quietness, O God, you steal upon our hearts. You were ever prone to meet us in silence and brokenness, and you are here now, speaking to us in the meagerness of our faith and through the fragility and weakness of our human condition. Accept us as we are, dear God, and help us to accept ourselves the same way. Forgive us our posturing and bravado, our pretending to be what we are not because we are afraid of not being accepted as we are. Help us to relax and be at home with you and with one another and with our selves. Take away, even for a few minutes, our loneliness and isolation from one another. Repair our trust in other people. Give us the energy we need to try again in life. Help us to take risks. Turn life into an adventure once more. Show us the road to service and give us hearts and minds eager to be on it. Hear our prayers for the sick and infirm of our community. Embrace with your gentle arms the lives of those who have lost loved ones in recent days or months, and make this holy season particularly full of meaning to them. Let us see all the beggars of the world who sit at our gates, whether for bread or for love, and minister to them in the name of Christ, whose birthday requires all this time to celebrate. Amen.

58

A Pastoral Prayer for a Time of Winter Storms

In the frozenness of the world around us, O God, we are aware of our need for warmth and shelter. We thank you for warm houses and offices and churches, for food and energy, and resources of transportation. We lift our prayers for people in need: for families without fuel, for those whose homes are inadequate for winter climates, for children without enough warm clothing, for workers without jobs, for old people without proper food to eat, for all who suffer from the lack of the things we take for granted. We remember too, O God, that there is a coldness of the spirit just as there is a frozenness of the earth, and that no matter how warm we are in the flesh we are not well off until our spirits too are warm. Teach us to care for our souls as we do for our bodies: to put on the warm vest of prayer and meditation; to wear the scarf of study and reflection; to don the coat of kindness and gentleness to others; to slip into the gloves of doing for others, and the boots of sharing what we have in a disciplined way; and to place on our heads the snug hat or scarf of an imagination devoted to you and your kingdom. Then we shall be warm indeed, sheltered from every wind of despair and fortified against the chill of loneliness. Nor, having prayed for the poor and ourselves, can we neglect those who are touched by coldness in other ways, especially the coldness of death. There is a numbness, dear God, among those who have lost loved ones in recent days and weeks. Give warmth of spirit to them, we ask; let the soft mantle of your loving-kindness fall on them, providing renewed circulation to their hopes and energies, and protecting them from the chill of distress and grief. Create in all of us that sense of warmth and comfort that comes from being together in the Body of Christ and drawing strength and meaning from our relationship. It is hard to be alone in the cold, O God; help us to be together, one with another and with you, for you are our warmth and our well-being, our eternal provider, world without end. Amen.

59

Almighty God, who in the winter of the year is able to make it summer in our hearts, we pray that we may enter into the life of faith and love that was taught to us by your Son Jesus. Help us to turn from all earthly idols—from confidence in our money and what it can buy, from pride in our positions and what they may mean to others, from trust in good health and its continuance, from addiction to pleasure and self-indulgence and sin—and to walk humbly in your gracious Spirit. Make us sober in our minds, clear-sighted, and able to see life from an eternal perspective. Let us, like the disciples of old, leave all in order to find everything. Show us the joy in serving others: the poor, who are always in need; the hungry, who never know comfort; the sick, who can take no pleasure in life; the untutored, who cannot read your Word; the unredeemed, who have not received you as Lord. Grant your peace to all of these, and to us as we are able to know and follow your will, which has been made known to us from ancient times in the life and ministry of Jesus Christ. Amen.

60

A Pastoral Prayer for Palm Sunday

O God, who has known the clamor of a thousand Palm Sundays and the disappointment of a million crucifixions, we bow in your presence as those who have both affirmed and denied you, and ask your forgiveness. Give us your grace, that we may learn to live in affirmation and not in denial. Let the Spirit that was in Christ Jesus our Lord be in us, that we may say "Abba, Father," and walk in your righteousness. Deliver us from false values, from selfish desire and the worship of things, that we may not waste our lives on goals and objects with no eternal significance. Guard us this week from betraying our Christ as Judas did, for a few pieces of silver or a promotion at the office or a quick thrill or a cheap victory over an enemy. Lead us daily to the garden of prayer, that we may empty ourselves and know your will and have the courage to do it. Strengthen us for the betrayals and crucifixions we face, that we may triumph through faith and love, and that we may know in our own flesh and hearts and minds the power of your resurrection. Grant health to the sickly and wholeness to the broken. Let grace overflow like a fountain in our lives, nurturing our affection for mercy and peace and goodness. And guide us into ministries of hearing and responding to all your little ones, in the name of Christ. Amen.

61
A Pastoral Prayer for Holy Week

O God, who has brought us once more to this Holy Week, in which we remember the ministry and suffering of our Lord, help us now to submerge our own needs and hurts and anxieties in his and learn of him. Show us by the resoluteness with which he accomplished your will how we too may live gracefully under pressure. Teach us by his example, when darkness and difficulty befall us, to gather our best friends around us and share our love without restraint. Enable us, when we are betrayed as he was betrayed, to continue to live with peace and equanimity. Guide us, when enemies taunt and life is cruelest, when we have encountered our own Calvaries of the spirit, to respond as positively as he did, blessing those who have used us falsely and committing our souls to you in steadfast faith. And when life ends, even in pain and separation, receive us then as you received him, renewing us by the everlasting resurrection of our total personalities, that we may dwell with him and you in the completeness of your Holy Spirit, and praise your name forever and ever, world without end. Amen.

62

A Pastoral Prayer for Easter Sunday

O God of history and God of love, whose Son Jesus died on a cross and was raised from the dead, we wait before you in the excitement of this Easter Day as those who would die to their sins and be brought to newness of life in him. Lower into the grave all selfishness, greed, and envy, all harmful desires and unworthy ambitions, and make to rise, as if by a miracle, the good in our hearts, the love we bear to other persons, and the wish we nourish to make the world a better place. As blossoms open in the springtime, confirming the continuity of life in the world of nature, bring flowering and openness to our personalities, that we may readily share ourselves and our possessions with one another, and participate even now in the kingdom that will know no end. Teach us to regard each day the hundreds of opportunities to see your presence in the people and places around us, and to live with joy and hope from moment to moment, as though this life were heaven itself. Make us channels of blessing and fulfillment for all the poor and unredeemed persons of the earth. And may the power that overcame death in the Lord Jesus at last overcome it completely in us as well, that we may rejoice with the saints in all the ages and proclaim your love eternally, time without end. Amen.

63
A Pastoral Prayer for Easter Sunday

Lord of Calvary and the Empty Tomb, we greet you! The world is different today because of you. The headlines may tell of wars and strikes and natural disasters, but we know the good news that Christ is risen! We are well acquainted with death and dying and grief, but we know you have vanquished death and broken its spell. Our lives are still embroiled in sin and failure and inadequacy, but you have given us meaning and purpose and new direction. There are days when we forget your power and fall into despair, but today we remember, and hope comes back. We came in doubt and disarray, but now we bow down in worship. We came like Thomas, wanting to see the nailprints and the wound in your side, but your presence is enough: we fall down and cry, "My Lord and my God!" Walk among us, Lord, and touch our troubled lives. Give hope to the hopeless, strength to the faltering, love to the lonely, honesty to the deceitful, consolation to the grieving, faith to the faithless. Let the radiance of your resurrected presence shine upon us as it shone upon your first disciples and make new persons of us as it did of them. Transform us from frightened, hesitant, uncommitted followers into people of fire and steel who know what they have seen and will follow it even unto death. Help us to spread the word of a passion that has come in and through us. Let this be your upper room, let this be your Emmaus road, let this be your seashore in the early morning. Walk among us and teach us to walk with you. Grant that no boy or girl, man or woman will leave here today without having stood in your presence and known it. For we have no other reason for being here. You alone have the words of eternal life, and you alone can call us into discipleship. Lord of Calvary and the Empty Tomb, we greet you! Make *our* worlds different, for your name's sake. Amen.

64
A Pastoral Prayer for Easter Sunday

O God, whose love was revealed at a cross and whose power was shown at an empty tomb, our hearts swell within us at the thought of your presence. We know that we live too often on the wrong side of Easter, worrying about things that are trivial in the light of the Resurrection of Christ. Forgive us for our lack of faith, and teach us to live more daringly, more expectantly, more joyfully. Let the discovery of the first Christians, that evil is doomed in the world, take hold of our minds and transform them into vessels of hope and excitement. Show us how to submerge our self-interests, which are small and unworthy, into confidence in your eternal kingdom, which will come despite wars and injustice, ignorance and prejudice, illness and death. Grant that we may become your agents of conversion and commitment in the world, feeding the hungry, clothing the poor, caring for the sick, and teaching the illiterate. Make the spirit of resurrection contagious among us, that we may honor our risen Lord in active discipleship. And grant that his name may ring out today in every nation, like the gladness of bells, calling men and women everywhere to the mystery of redemption in the community of faith. For yours is the kingdom and the power and the glory forever. Amen.

65
A Pastoral Prayer for Easter Sunday

O God, whose presence is like the sunrise and whose love is a fresh breeze blowing in our hearts, we remember again today the empty tomb and the angels and the excitement of Jesus' followers, and confess that we too want to believe in the Resurrection. In a world of towering buildings and busy freeways, we want to believe in the simple things that make life meaningful. In a world of big business and the hard sell and saturation advertising, we want to believe in the truth that sets people free. In a world of endless bureaucracy, where it is hard to get anything done, we want to believe in the love that cuts through red tape and reaches us immediately. In a world that is busy and complicated and stressful and even impossible, we want to believe that Jesus died for our sins, that he rose from the grave, and that even now he lives as our Lord and Master and calls us into his service. Let your Spirit come upon our lives to reorder them in the direction of wholeness and obedience. Teach us to be sacrificial, caring more for things that are eternal than for momentary pleasures and satisfactions. Reinstill in us a sense of responsibility for the earth, and for the human community that inhabits it. Help us to be neighbors to the poor and unfortunate. Give us leaders who are wise and generous. Let our church be a giving church, a channel of your blessing as it reaches out to the homeless and the hungry, the illiterate and the displaced, the confused and the lonely. May the spirit and sensibility that were in Christ Jesus be in us as well, motivating us to lives of lovingkindness. And may the earth resound this day with the news of Christ's victory over death, bringing hope to those who live in prisons of any kind, whether of despair or illness or cynicism or unhappiness, for yours is the kingdom that shall never die and the love that shall never end. Amen.

66
A Pastoral Prayer for Easter Sunday

O Lord of the darkest night and Lord of the brightest morning; O Lord of the deepest heartache and Lord of the greatest ecstasy; O Lord of the sorrow of death and Lord of the power of life; we greet you as those who have seen your morning and known your ecstasy and experienced your life; we praise your name above every name, both in heaven and on earth and under the earth, and honor you both with our voices and with our spirits, that sing aloud in glorious harmony for all your mercies and all your greatness and all your love. There are extraordinary times in our lives, of which this is one, when the veil between this life and the one beyond it is so thin that, as the poet said, "to pass from one to the other were easy"; when doubt grows faint and belief grows strong; when the world fades from view and heaven becomes our dearest reality; when self becomes all but meaningless and your divine presence becomes everything! Teach us to walk each day, we ask, in reverence for what we know and feel at this moment. Let your presence be preferred above every delight of the self; let heaven become the pattern by which we test and judge this world; let belief overcome all doubt, and direct our feet in pathways of light and joy. We pray for the continuing power of Easter to reach into the lives of all our people and all our visitors, healing the sick, giving sight to blinded hearts, raising up tired lives, mending broken relationships, comforting those who grieve, and inspiring those who have been depressed. Grant that our church shall be the church of the Resurrection, living and teaching and proclaiming the truth of your Spirit. Call those who worship you today to a renewed ministry in your name. Mold us into a powerful instrument for affecting the quality of life in this community, uplifting goodness and defeating crime, promoting fellowship and denying prejudice, preaching the good news of the kingdom and destroying evil. We do not ask to be exempted from suffering; we ask only to suffer with joy and expectancy, knowing that this present age shall one day give way to your glorious eternity, and that we shall reign with you, triumphant in the heavens, new world without end. Amen.

67

Why is it, O God, that we hear you better in the silence than when we are speaking? Is it that when we are full of ourselves there is no room for you? Teach us to be quiet more often, and to listen. Speak to us in the sky and the earth and the rivers and creeks and the trees and stones you have made. Speak to us in the city streets and the buildings and the factories and the machines and the wonders our hands have fashioned with the gifts you have given us. Speak to us in our relationships: in our families and friendships and clubs and jobs and churches and classes. Speak to us in our bodies: these wonderful, intricate, perplexing, and eloquent encasements of feeling and perception. And speak to us in our faith journeys, which wind not only through our lives but through the lives of others, twisting and turning, uphill and down, over plains and mountains, beside still waters and through turbulent floods. Help us to hear you calling out to us in the evening news, in the voices of our children, in the plight of our cities, in the opportunities for our planet, in the desperation of emerging nations. Let the cry that reached the ears of the Apostle, "Come over and help us," reach us as well, and let us answer with our talents and our imaginations and our money and our presence. Speak, dear God, and let your servants hear. Whisper your call into our hearts. Cure our indifference, heal our brokenness, overcome our separateness. Bind us to the future you are building, and let us embrace your design for our lives. For yours is the kingdom that will never end and the love that will never be exhausted, though time be forever. Amen.

68

You exist at the center of everything, O God; you *are* the center of everything, and our lives cohere only as they find centeredness in you. Forgive us our tendency to wander off or away, and never give up on us. Keep bringing us back to the center, returning us to the fold, welcoming us at your table. Help us to understand our concentricity with you, our need to be focused on you, to have all our thoughts and activities brought into orbit with you, in order that we may live with full humanity and highest freedom. And now, as we feel ourselves being restored to that inner unity with you, hear the concerns of our hearts for those we love—for those enduring pain or suffering—for our president and other leaders—for the nation's schools—for all teachers—for our members who face difficult times—for our visitors—for the affairs of our own lives—and for the world at large—Give peace in our time, O God, and renew your spirit in the earth, that we may praise you with all our hearts and worship you with everything we have. Through Jesus Christ our Lord. Amen.

69

We are gathered here from many homes, O God, and our hopes and dreams and needs may appear to be very different. Yet we are all aware of our deep hunger for truth and beauty and peace and love. Whatever our backgrounds and lifestyles, we know we depend on you for our very life and happiness. Help us therefore to find our way to the center of life and mystery where you are, and to lay aside all the foolish ambitions and expectations that cloud our thinking and impede our progress toward that center. Even though we are shy about making commitments, give us such a vision of the life we could enjoy in you that we shall not hesitate to worship you with all we have and are, and to follow in the way you show us for the remainder of our days. We lift up for your special care today friends and loved ones who are ill or struggling or unhappy; let the divine presence rest upon them to give them rest and joy and peace. We remember our young people and invoke your continuing love and guidance in their lives. Bless our president, the cabinet, and the members of our congress, that they may transcend political interests and ideology for the good of this republic, and indeed of all the world. Give all of us fertile imaginations for envisioning what we can do to amend the ills and injustices of our entire world; and endow us with kindness and gentleness in dealing with one another and even with those who are hostile to us. Through Christ Jesus our Lord. Amen.

70

O God, who made lilacs and dandelions, roses and thistles, we thank you for both, for the delightful varieties and contrarieties in our existence. Save us, we pray, from valuing one more than the other and thus becoming critical of the creation. Help us instead to glory in what our eyes behold and our ears hear, and to live like children in the sheer excitement of being alive, in the wonder that there is anything at all and not nothing. Teach us the deep joy of loving one another, of caring for people who are quite unlike ourselves, and for those in our immediate society. Make of us one communion: the old and the young, the prince and the pauper, the beautiful swan and the ugly duckling, the worker and the sluggard, the athlete and the paraplegic, the whole and the afflicted, the powerful and the marginalized, the proper and the improper, even the good and the bad. Let us not judge others, lest in so doing, we judge ourselves. Give rest and happiness to all our visitors, and traveling mercies to those who travel. Anoint with special blessings those who were recently married in this church. Attend our friends and relatives who have been recently deceased. And grant that each of us, in the course of this time together, may become so aware of your touching us, of your spirit brushing almost insensibly against our own hearts and spirits, that we shall be freshly encouraged to live and work and play with zest and vigor in the hours and days ahead. Through Jesus Christ our Lord, who lives and reigns with you forever and ever. Amen.

71

O God, who in your divine sense of comedy and ecology created giant redwoods and tiny forget-me-nots, hippopotami and hummingbirds, mammoth sharks and diminutive tadpoles, great rough lumberjacks and delicate little children, we praise you for the glory of all that is, and for the privilege of living in such a wondrous, inviting world. We thank you for the faith of those who have gone before us, and for the sense of the transcendent they have bequeathed to us. Grant that we shall not be remiss in conveying their understandings of value and purpose to those who follow us. Teach us to live each day as cherishing love and honor and dependability above all personal status and material prosperity. Remind us when we go astray of the sadness we produce in the hearts of all the saints and angels gathered around your throne. Imbue us with a strong desire to bring healing and justice to everyone in the world around us, especially those who cannot claim it for themselves. Use our imaginations to design important new systems, and our hearts to conceive of ways to make love supreme in our midst, and our arms to embrace the neglected, the lonely, and the unlovely. Send the spirit of your Son Jesus among us to challenge us once more with his devotion and sacrifice, and to recreate in us the soul of the early church. And let your name be uppermost in our minds at all times, morning, noon, and night, for you are worthy of all praise and honor, O God, forever and ever, world without end. Amen.

72

O God, whose ways are higher than ours and whose love is never quenched, so that the power that shaped the universe and the galaxies continues even now to mold and alter our destinies, we wait before you as those who are completely dependent on your grace, joyfully submitting ourselves to the only will and mind able to guarantee our happiness. Teach us to find our peace in you, and, rejecting all other goods and priorities, so to immerse ourselves in your spirit that we perfectly reflect your care and desire, not only for our lives, but for the world around us. Make us thoughtful stewards of all we appear to possess, even our relationships with one another. Help us to regard one another so highly that we would interpose our own bodies, if necessary, to shield the other from hurt or disease. Bless the visitors among us, that they may find help and healing in this company and return upon their way refreshed and cheered by having been here. Tend our sick and distressed, and let them find health and wholeness in you. Enable us all to find joy in the tasks we do, and satisfaction in following a God who also works, who has created the worlds, and who is still engaged at accomplishing your will in every heart. For you are a great God, and worthy to be praised, through Jesus Christ our Lord. Amen.

73

O God, whose breath revives the flowers and the trees in the springtime and is able to make us live again, though we were dead in sins and trespasses, we worship you in quietness and prayerfulness. Speak to us, though our hearts have been cold and selfish. Touch us, though we have recoiled from your service. Embrace us, though we have resisted your love. Help us to live and to grow again. Let new life course through our tired and dormant ways of being in the world. Send your Spirit upon us to lead us into new relationships, new engagements, new energy, and new hope. Make us throb with your vitality and love. Let the despondent become joyous, the afflicted whole, and the aggrieved lighthearted. Give us your peace, O God, that is full and beautiful as a garden, and let us scatter its seeds everywhere in the world, until all the kingdoms of this earth become the kingdom of our Christ. Amen.

74

O Lord, whom the very stones would praise if we did not, forgive us for our neglect of you. We do not begin our days as we ought, under the sign of your cross. We do not live the hours as we ought, in constant remembrance of your grace. We do not use your gifts as we ought, for the redemption of the world around us. Let your Spirit come upon us and make us aware of your presence here. Teach us to live tremblingly, in awe and wonder, marveling at the riches of our surroundings and bowing our heads in submission to your love. Put away from us all greed, resentment, and wrong desire. Let our souls flower in gentleness, peace, and goodwill. Help us to discern what is wrong in our lives and in the corporate structures of our world, and to apply our energies to making your kingdom come on earth as it is in heaven. Send healing upon our sick and comfort upon those who are distressed. Grant wisdom to the leaders of our world and relief to all who are poor or hungry or imprisoned. Let forgiveness overwhelm us as a flood, cleansing us of evil and raising us to new life in the blessed community. For your name's sake. Amen.

75

O God, whose hand is seen in the coming of spring and whose love is experienced in the laughter of children, the smile of a friend, the sense of well-being we feel when we sit in church surrounded by light and music and prayer, we thank you for this day and this moment of quietness, and for the pause from our labors and the richness of your Word and the table spread before us. Help us to be so keenly aware of your presence that it will change our lives: that it will make our burdens lighter, our way easier, our hopes stronger, our sense of love and security deeper and more meaningful. Grant peace to those who are most troubled, comfort to those who grieve, and encouragement to those who have been disappointed or discouraged. Teach us to live from day to day with a sense of wonder for the world you have made, and to learn from wonder love, that we may be your ministering hands to poor and hungry and diseased persons in every nation. Give gentleness and wisdom to the leaders of our world, and let the vision of your heavenly kingdom become the model for our earthly friendships, preserving joy and trust at the heart of every relationship, through Jesus Christ our Lord. Amen.

76

A Pastoral Prayer for Independence Day

We confess to you, O God, the many sins of our nation: the sin of pride, when we have believed ourselves superior to others; the sin of despair, when we have thought ourselves worse than others; the sin of greed, when we have sought to be the richest of nations; the sin of intolerance, when we have despised the ways of other groups or races; the sin of wrongdoing, when we have taken the land of those who were here before us, and enslaved the people of other nations to work the land; the sin of not caring, when we have built fortunes on the labor and suffering of others without giving them their due; the sin of poisoning the earth and the sky and the rivers for our own selfish benefits; the sin of making war when it wasn't necessary; the sin of acting expediently and not compassionately in the world; the sin of pretending to be religious and faithful to you when we weren't and aren't. Send renewal to our nation, O God. Let the Spirit that was in Christ Jesus be in us now, converting our natures to yours, that we may truly love you and the world you have made, and that we may love our country for its great ideals of justice and peace and righteousness more than for any selfish reason. For your name's sake. Amen.

77

You have shown us, O God, what is good: to do justice, to love mercy, and to walk humbly with you. Forgive us, we pray, for all our failures to be good and to have our own lives recreated in your image. Repair and renew us now, we ask, and help us to recommit ourselves to you and your kingdom. Grant us a sense of the church as Jesus envisioned it, not as it has often become, and help us to strive together to be that higher, purer church, loving one another without respect to rank or station, caring for those in need, living with honesty and honor, and worshiping at our center the living Christ, who chose the church to be his heavenly bride, his consort for the ages. Nor would we neglect to invoke a blessing upon our visitors today, whose presence is always important to us; help them to feel our genuine sense of hospitality and our desire to be of service to them in any way we can. Walk with all who have been recently married in this place, that their lives may be full and happy. Use us to minister to those who hurt or carry heavy burdens of any kind, that we may all share the bread of the gospel in equal manner. And grant that our worship may blend today with that of countless congregations around the globe, acknowledging your mercy and praising your multifold grace, for you are worthy to be known and praised in every place, O God most high, our creator and our redeemer. Amen.

78

O God, whom we see in every summer flower and flowing stream, teach us to see you as well in the haggard faces of the old, the gaunt or bloated bodies of the poor, and the imploring eyes of children. Help us who are called by your name to have your vision of the world of the future, as a place where the lion lies down with the lamb, the person with two coats shares with the person who has none, and everyone takes care of children and the aged. Release us from our bondage to self-interest—worrying about what we shall eat, or what we shall wear, or how we shall look to others who are watching us—and guide us into the freedom of your Spirit, where we shall be relaxed and confident and supportive of others. Teach us to number our days as gifts that are given for our work and enjoyment, that we may never treat them as obstacles to be overcome or burdens to be endured. Show us the excitement of time and ideas and dreams shared together, and enable us to be a community in Christ, whose body we are. Grant a special capacity for grace to those who are ill today in body or spirit, and let their very sense of your presence become the bonus of difficult days. Send wisdom upon the leaders of our world, that they may better cope with the confusion and complexity of the many problems facing the nations, and bring us all into greater sensitivity to the needs of those living under poverty or injustice. Now let your Holy Spirit overpower us as we worship, blotting out sin that would blind us to your glory and raising us to the newness of life that is in Christ Jesus our Lord, to whom be praise and obedience forever and ever. Amen.

79

O God of all mercies, giver of life and love and grace, we lift our voices in thanksgiving to you for everything that fills our hearts with joy: for the smell of bread baking in the oven; for little children lifting their arms to be taken; for flowers blooming beside the way; for telephone calls from friends and loved ones; for a cool drink in the heat of the day; for restful sleep without burdens or anxieties; for the memory of good times; for the touch of those who are dear; for the hope of tomorrow and what it will bring. Yet we are mindful of many whose lives are troubled and restless: people who are unhappy in marriage and feel betrayed by life; children who are the victims of marital strife and divorce, and live in a jungle of fear and confusion and self-reproach; friends who are ill and live under the shadow of pain and hurt and separation; people who have experienced the loss of dear ones and now feel that all life has lost its meaning and purpose; people who have lost jobs or homes or self-respect or reputation or a sense of direction and wonder if they will ever find their way again. Hasten the day of your kingdom, dear God, that all humanity may see it together and find relief from the burdens of living. And in the meantime, help us to be followers of Christ, who taught us how to live as if the kingdom were here now, sharing what we have with other persons and loving one another for no reason at all, except that you first loved us and Christ died to redeem us from emptiness and loneliness and evil. In his name we pray. Amen.

80

O God, whose grace is in the shadows as well as the sunshine, and who meets us on every road of life with open arms, we thank you for the community of love and fellowship in Jesus Christ—for the heritage of faith, for the biblical word, for schools and seminaries and churches, for this congregation, for your Spirit working over us and in us and through us, bringing us closer and closer to your will and teaching us to share our lives and possessions with one another and the world. We are sorry for the obstructionism we have practiced, resisting your Word and your Spirit, trying to have things our own way and making a mess of ourselves and our relationships. Help us to be more open, more surrendered, more giving. Let the commitment and generosity that marked our Lord become ours as well. Teach us to weep with one another, laugh with one another, and join arms against the sea of troubles that often threatens to sweep us away. And let us not only love one another here in this church and this community, but love our brothers and sisters in South Africa and Afghanistan and Nicaragua and India and Russia and Argentina—wherever human beings are imprisoned, impoverished, mistreated, or misled. Let the world for which you gave your only begotten Son become the true sphere of our love and concern and responsibility. And now, as we approach your throne in worship, let your healing power fall upon your children who are ill or depressed, and let your spirit of peace be upon their families and friends. Grant an increase of faith and comfort to those whose loved ones have recently entered the doorway of eternal life, and enable us all to orient our hearts more successfully toward that significant occasion in our own lives, and away from the tawdry and ephemeral desires of this worldly existence. Save our children from harm and draw their spirits into your keeping. Open our eyes to see you waiting for us on the roadways of life and let us run forward to meet you, lost in wonder, love, and praise. Through Jesus Christ our Lord. Amen.

81

O God, whom we know better when are being quiet than when we are speaking, and when we are bowed down in gratitude than when we walk about consumed by pride, we thank you for the sense of your presence that enlivens and enriches our understanding of the world around us. Without you, life is dull and shallow and unworthy of the energy we spend on it. You give us a feeling of stability and continuity, of depth and meaning. You comfort us when we are tired and afraid. You lift our spirits when we are discouraged. You accompany us through the valley of the shadow of death. Surely your name is above every name, and we ought happily to praise it morning, noon, and night. Make this an hour of renewal and recommitment for us. Bless each of our visitors with joy and refreshment for their daily living. Care for our friends and loved ones who suffer any illness or indisposition. Consecrate our imaginations to the task of helping this world to become interfaced with your kingdom, so that the hungry are fed, the sick are healed, the children are taught, the elderly are comforted, and the neglected are welcomed and loved. And grant that we shall not rest in our own comfort and thereby fail to make the mystery of Christ and the fellowship of the Holy Spirit known in every heart, before Christ himself shall come again as our Lord and Judge. Amen.

82

O God, who changes rivers in their courses and alters the paths of distant stars, come now and direct us into new ways of thinking and living that will bring us to perfect joy in you. Help us to be willing to risk everything in pursuit of your kingdom. Speak vibrantly to those among us whose minds are tired or bored or locked in routine. Rekindle happiness in those whose hearts have been heavy with loss and grief. Restore sparkle to the eyes of those who feel defeated or broken. Set the cross once more in our midst and remind us of the life that springs out of death and the hope that rises from despair. Let all our problems and illnesses be but a turning in the road that brings us back to you, and then bestow new energy, new under-standing, new imagination upon us. We commit to your care our children, that they may know and love you; our elderly, that they may rejoice in your strength and care; our visitors, that they may prosper in all they do; our friends and loved ones who are ill, that they may trust in you for healing; the leaders of our world, that they may bow down to you and your will for the nations; and our church, that it may serve you with gladness and joy. Through Jesus Christ our Lord. Amen.

83

Into the clutter of our everyday lives, O Lord, you come with your heavenly order; into the weakness you come with your strength; into the sin you come with your holiness. Give us the grace to receive you now, to open the doors of our beings and invite you in, not just over the threshold but into the inmost parts, the upper rooms and lower rooms, the nooks and crannies and closets. Dwell in us, O Lord, that we may glow with your light and pulsate with your presence. Let the peace that has stilled the hearts of saints in all the ages still our hearts as well. Let the courage that has animated them animate us. Let the imagination that has possessed them possess us, in order that we may transcend what we have known of ourselves and devote ourselves truly to glorifying your name in all the earth. Give each of us a feeling for history, and for the way your hand is at work within it, shaping it finally toward the purposes of your kingdom. Let Christ be in our midst today, steadying those who have lost their footholds in life, encouraging those who have forgotten their way, comforting those who have buried loved ones, and inspiring all of us to love and hope and sacrifice. Gather up our spirits in your Holy Spirit, that we may experience oneness and unanimity of purpose, and that we may become a sweet offering to you upon the altar of the world, living and dying in behalf of the poor and neglected, for whom Christ himself gave his life upon the cross. Amen.

84

O God, in whose will is our peace and in whose peace is our salvation, we thank you for the abundance of our lives this day: for azure skies and blossoming flowers; for coffee and toast and cereal; for the comfort of old clothes and the excitement of new ones; for church towers and winding streets; for the touch and smile of friends; for the voices and faces of children; for hymn and prayer and scripture; for altar and candlelight; for bowed heads and quiet moments. Visit us with the grace of recognition, that we may see you in all these things and thousands more. Fill our hearts with your Spirit and redeem us from mere ordinary existence.

Bless all the dear friends who are gathered with us today, and attend to the needs of their lives. Give strength to the weak, patience to the fretful, healing to the sick, and comfort to the mournful. Bestow grace on the very elderly, and also on the very young. Teach us to number our days and apply them to wisdom. Enable us to sense the importance of our fellowship in you, and to strive to enhance it with never failing love and gentleness. And grant that we may all walk taller and straighter, and with a spring in our step, for having laid bare our souls in worship and lingered in your presence this beautiful day. Through Christ our Savior. Amen.

85

We pause, O God, and in pausing find life. Here, where you meet us, is the center of everything. Here, a light dawns, a fountain springs up, the heart is moved. Here, we find inspiration, hope, purpose, fellowship, love. Here, you bless the work of the secretary who has labored all week at a cluttered desk, of a manager who has struggled to make a business successful, of a housekeeper who has fought the good fight against dirt and disorder, of a doctor who has seen an endless stream of sick and disabled persons, of a teacher who has advanced courageously against a wall of darkness, of a student who has caught glimpses of light and tried to follow them. You are God, and in that one realization our lives are changed, now and forever. You are God, and when we bow before you an energy flows into our lives, a spirit beyond any spirit we have ever known. Teach us to pause before you and find life, not only here, but wherever we are. Let this simple act transform the world of our engagement, because it has transformed the way we see the world. Anoint our president and his staff with uncommon wisdom. Grant that the present disorders of our society may soon be given a new order that reflects the teachings of your kingdom. Give hope and encouragement to our sick, and healing of spirit to those who have said good-bye to loved ones. Show us how to be better ministers to one another, and to the poor and homeless of our society. Help us to reflect upon those sayings and writings that will inspire us to right living, and to pause often upon our journeys to be filled with your presence. Here we offer our worship to you, in song and prayer and thought and silence; accept it as our meager gift, and let us be transformed in the giving of it, for yours are the kingdom and the power and the glory forever. Amen.

86

O God, in whom there is a fullness to supply every need, we are here this morning because we are incomplete without you. You have made us for yourself and our hearts are restless until they find rest in you. There are times when we think we are adequate alone, but then illness strikes or a pipe breaks and floods the house or someone we know gets AIDS and we remember how limited we are, how lost and limited without you. Forgive us for the pride and self-confidence that have stood in our way and help us to find joy in your arms again today. We hold before you especially our friends and loved ones who face particular dangers or difficulties and bear unusually heavy loads this day: those in hospitals; those recovering from operations or illness at home; those who travel; those facing difficult decisions; those beginning new jobs; those with domestic problems; those with declining physical powers or increasing mental confusion; those trying to overcome addictions of one kind or another; those dealing with a lack of faith; those suffering from hunger or homelessness; those who feel useless and unappreciated; those who are tired and overextended; and those who are simply confused and cannot find their way in life. You love us, O God; we know that. Help us to find a connection to you that is meaningful to us, whatever our needs and problems. Let us hear some word, let us feel some touch, let your Spirit settle upon us and give us peace. May the way before us become plain and may our strength be equal to the journey. Guide our president and his advisors, and all other leaders of our nation and the world. Help them to see beyond personal advantages and even beyond immediate advantages to their nations, and to plant the seeds for a more just and moral world tomorrow. Now bless the fellowship we enjoy in this place, the sense of being pilgrims together on the way of life, and help us worthily to praise and magnify your name in prayer and song and deed, through Jesus Christ our Lord. Amen.

87

O God who made the heavens and the earth, we extol your name for the many beauties and marvels of our existence: the sea filled with fish, the sky of clouds and birds, the mountains fringed with trees, the valleys rich with fruit and grain, the easy smiles of old friends, the sense of belonging in home and church, our minds at peace when they are stayed on you. Teach us today to see beyond the limits of yesterday's vision, to care beyond the boundaries of yesterday's caring, to have faith beyond the scope of former faith. Let Christ rise in us as he rose from the dead, and open the musty rooms of our lives to freshness and vitality. Give peace to those whose hearts are troubled and joy to those with thoughts depressed. Grant companionship to the lonely and comfort to the bereaved. Bestow confidence upon those who face trials and difficult times. Show mercy on the wayward and restore us all to the path of righteousness. Guide our president and other leaders of government in this season of re-examination and decision making, and make of us a kinder, gentler nation, truly qualified to lead the world in decades to come. Let your blessings fill the hearts of our visitors and let them not be strangers among us. Reveal yourself to us in your Word, and in the very atmosphere of this beautiful sanctuary, and let our lives be changed in this hour to reflect your glory, O Creator, Lord, and Holy Spirit, infinite in power, yet warm and loving in every way. Amen.

88

O God, whose mercy falls upon us like a mantle, covering all our sins and anxieties, we thank you for sanctuary: for sanctuary from the past and all our mistakes; for sanctuary from a world that is often hard and confusing; for sanctuary from fear and worry; for sanctuary from busyness and work. Help us to rest here for the hour and be restored for our journeys. Teach us to be aware of our fellow pilgrims and the burdens they bring to this place. Enable us to hear one another's stories and to recognize what a common humanity we share. We celebrate our origins—Europeans and Asians, Central Americans and North Americans, blacks and whites, reds and yellows, all made one in Christ. We praise you for the church and its wide canopy in the world. Bless your Word this day, that it may be heard in every country of the globe. Open our ears, that we too may hear and feast upon it. We thank you for this church and its ministry. Let this be a day of gratitude and celebration, when we remember not the difficulties and demands of life, but its grace notes and delights. We know that you are a God of compassion and healing, and we pray for compassion and healing for those who are ill or lonely or neglected. We lift up the individual needs and problems all over this room—people, situations, feelings. Hear our prayer for them. Now bind us together under the long shadow of the cross and help us to hear the promise of the Resurrection. As Christ is with us, let us never be afraid. As you love us, let us never think we are alone. And let your kingdom come on earth as it is in heaven, that everywhere may be sanctuary; through him who lived and died and lives forever. Amen.

89

O God of morning light and God of evening shadows, we thank you for life and all its fullness; for plants, deep green, upon the soil; for oxygen, rich and vital in the lungs; for seas of fish and plains of cattle; for places of comfort and familiarity; for people's faces, black and white, and bronzed and tawny; for children's laughter, lilting and carefree; for language, clear, expressive, and poetic; for song, uplifting and melodic; for faith, supportive and inviting. Teach us to live simply from day to day, feeling the breeze, hearing the birds, caring about one another. Let the strain and anxiety in our bodies flow away, and let love prevail. Show us how to care for the earth and for its children. Help us to value sacrifice, both in ourselves and in our nation. Stop us from running after goods that do not enlarge us and wealth that does not enrich us. Give us pleasure in kind deeds and thoughtful words and creative minds. Enable us to bear suffering, to share enthusiasm, and to forgive our enemies. Let our children be filled with your Spirit, that they may live in gentleness and love. Make our leaders sensitive to your will for our future, and our people eager to follow them with patriotism and respect. Give grace to our media, that they may guide us in constructive ways, and bless all teachers, that they may be endowed with strength, wisdom, and courage. Finally, let your church hear and teach the gospel of Christ in all its power and fullness, that people may be saved and your kingdom come, for all goodness and mercy are in your hands and you are our God forever. Amen.

90

O Lord most beautiful, we thank you for all the beautiful things in the world: for clear, blue skies, for tall pine trees, for tiny flowers and great mountains, for people's faces, and their smiles. O Lord most holy, we bless you for all the holy things we experience: for churches and cloisters, hallowed by people's prayers; for altars and sacraments, that make us catch our breath; for children's rooms, filled with love and imagination; for empty schoolrooms, where life has been; for sacred battlegrounds where cannon and horses are heard no more. O Lord most loving, we stretch our arms to you for all the loving persons we have ever known: for parents who held us and sang to us and felt content because we were theirs; for friends who accepted us as we were and did not feel the need to change us; for teachers who saw potential in us and tried to lure it out; for ministers who saw Christ in us; for husbands or wives who have cared for us more than they cared for themselves; for children who will never cease to love us, even when we are gone. We hold before you, O Lord, all things and people not beautiful or holy or loving, and ask your mercy on them. Let your redemptive care reach out to enfold them, and recreate them in your image. Make all things one in your power and love, and teach us to love them too, that we may be complete with them, for Jesus' sake. Amen.

91

O Lord, life is so beautiful, and you have filled it with such wonderful sights and sounds and people. Why do we often live in dread of the day ahead, or anesthetized to the glory of the present moment? Surely it is because we lose our sense of your presence in all that is, and see only the bareness and poverty of things in themselves. Teach us to covet your presence, and to seek it with all our hearts. Lead us into daily acts of prayer and reflection, that would make you more real to us. Show us how to find you in other persons—in the children who skip past us on the sidewalk, in the old man pushing a grocery basket, in the young couples chatting in a restaurant, in the elderly patients waiting in the doctor's office. Can it be, O God, that the final sin is to die without having lived? Restore us to a sense of passion and caring. Help us to share what we have with others, and to find joy and excitement in what we feel as we do it. Let Christ reside in us, as he did in the lives of those Galilean fishermen and tax collectors. Use us to reclaim the world that has been too busy and self-indulgent to notice you. Let the gift of our love become the balm that soothes hurt and wounded souls. Speak through us to the heart that grieves and the life that has been abused, and make this church a place of renewal and hope, through Jesus Christ our Lord. Amen.

92

O Lord, who could have made a world where no roses had thorns and no human beings hungered or turned to crime or made war on others, yet chose to involve us in perfecting our environment and our destiny, we are here to listen and find your direction for our living. We cannot live properly by ourselves. As hard as we try, we cannot think or act alone without taking the wrong road and getting into trouble. The perfect world exists only in your mind, O Lord, and we must consult you regularly in order to go about building it. When we wait quietly before you, as we have now, a new perspective on everything emerges. Our problems are no longer in the world outside us, but in our own hearts and minds. Therefore, we pray for our sin to be removed and forgiven. Our ambitions are no longer for personal gain and promotion, but for love and joy and relationship. Help us to be willing to surrender ourselves. Our commitment is no longer to the values of Wall Street or Madison Avenue or Hollywood, but to the hungry and the poor and the illiterate and the diseased and the displaced. Enable us to contribute to the struggle for justice and sufficiency for all. Our desire is no longer to be a church of glory and renown in the community, but to be a fellowship of those who fall down before the Lord of glory. Give us true humility before Christ and our calling to follow him. Bless with a sense of your presence all who have gathered here today—the tired, the broken, the bereaved, the rebellious, the resentful, the spoiled, and the selfish—and convert us into simple, empty vessels waiting to be filled by your love. Grant that even our visitors may not feel like strangers here, but that all together we shall experience being caught up in your Spirit and shown the world you want to exist and set free from our bondage in order to serve such a world. To that end, come, O holy One, touch our eyes, our mouths, our hands, our hearts, and our feet, that we may be wholly yours, and that this may be one of the finest hours of our lives, through Jesus Christ. Amen.

93

O God, whose heart beats with an almost tangible rhythm in a place like this, we come before you in awe and wonder, that you should be in love with us. You have known our inner beings, and the muddle we have made of things—the relationships we have failed to maintain, the gifts we have squandered, the bodies we have abused, the mysteries we have ignored, the Christ we have spurned—yet you have continued to care for us and to be there when we needed you. We praise you for Christ and his teachings—for the light that came among us, for the blessings that still flow from his life and ministry, death and resurrection. Remind us, O Lord, that we are people of the Resurrection, that we were formed for life, not death, and joy, not despair. Grant that wherever your church is gathered today there may be a sense of triumph and eternity. Let your eternal peace reign this morning in the lives of those who have surrendered loved ones in recent days; make them aware of the everlasting arms that support them, and constantly gather together all the saints whom death has taken. Bestow hope and quietness of spirit on all who wait for death; let the joy that is set before them far outweigh the sadness they feel in parting from loved ones here. Comfort us in all partings, even in this life. Let peace continue to break out in the world, overcoming natural tendencies to war and corruption. Help us to side with Christ against hate and hypocrisy and injustice. Make us your servants to the poor and hungry, the broken and disfavored; and let your kingdom come on earth, as it is in heaven; through your everlasting Spirit. Amen.

94

In the beauty of this place, O Lord, and in the quietness of our hearts, we know you better—and know ourselves better—than almost anywhere else. We feel your majesty in the pomp of processions. We sense your mystery in the light of candles and the height of the arches. We know your love in the smiles and touch of friends. We learn your will in the Word that is read and preached. We are moved to commitment by the hymns and anthems, and by the stirring music of a mighty instrument. Let this experience become normative, O God, and change our lives for all the rest of living. We lift before you now all our brothers and sisters who come with special cares or needs: some with worries about money or property; some with concerns about children or parents; some hungry for love and understanding; some tired of jobs or school; some fearful of life and its many demands; some yearning for change; *all* needing to see your face, to hear your voice, to feel your touch in their lives. Show yourself to us in this hour, O God. Let there be a strong sense of your presence. Walk the aisles, and let the hem of your garment brush us as you pass. Make mystery come back to our lives. Make joy and hope return. Make peace fill our souls. We pray for our great country—our broken country—and for statesmen and judges who try to lead us; for Congress, with its enormous task; for police and civil servants; for teachers and administrators and social workers and doctors and nurses and ministers and attorneys and business managers. Help us to solve the great problems facing our society: to rid our land of drugs and crime; to teach our people to read and to care; to think beyond war and pride and competition; to feed the hungry and heal the sick; to provide a place for the homeless and work for the jobless; to restore dignity and gentleness and worth to every life; to embody the teachings of Jesus in our corporate structures, in our laws, and in our way of behavior. Give strength to your church and grace to your ministers. Let the cross of Christ be lifted over us, and let the power of his kingdom bind us together in love and purpose, for you are our God and we are your people, now and evermore. Amen.

95

O God, whose kindness to us has taken forms we have never known and visited us in ways we did not see, we thank you for your countless mercies: for safety in traveling when some danger loomed; for return to health when disease threatened; for the smell of rain on dry pavement; for flowers that polkadot the landscape; for friends who rescue us from loneliness; for family members who stand by us in times of adversity; for a country where we are protected by law; for churches that still teach the ways of faith; for books that embody reflections and ideas; for Bibles that impart sacred history and understanding; for teachers who shape our lives; for work that ennobles life; for sleep that restores; for play that rejuvenates; for prayer that sustains. Forgive us, we pray, for ever taking anything for granted, and not acknowledging that you are the giver of every good and perfect gift. We hold before you today friends and loved ones who are ill; families in which there is anxiety or trouble; persons who are out of work; children having difficulty in school; adults who cannot read; people addicted to drugs; relatives of those addicted to drugs; persons contemplating crimes; persons in prison; persons experiencing burnout in work or faith or family life; those who are handicapped or whose health is debilitated in any way; those whose lives are painful or joyless; those who are out of communication with you. Grant that your Spirit may move among us in this place, generating new faith, healing wounds, causing fellowship, and filling hearts with joy and love. Teach us to share with one another the wonderful gifts you have given us, and then, encouraged by a common spirit of generosity, to reach beyond these walls with love and service and gifts for others. Let the vision of wholeness and commitment that was in Christ be in us also, and let your name be glorified here and in all the earth, for yours are the kingdom and the power and the glory forever. Amen.

96

The world is not an easy place, O Lord. It is filled with deceit and betrayal, envy and sloth, hardship and bureaucracy. Yet it is the world you have made, and the world you are still struggling to make, with great stretches of beauty and little pockets of grace and affirmation. We yearn for the day when all the kingdoms of this world will have become the kingdom of our Christ and all the difficulties in human relationships will have given way before your heavenly love. Teach us even now to begin living in this future mode, forgiving our enemies, rising graciously above our troubles, and seeking the good of others, not of ourselves. Remind us of the great history of faith, and all the men and women who have triumphed over their adversities to glorify your name; and of the place of the church in the centuries, as a gathering of those who love and care for one another, and who respond to your Word as a living presence in our midst. We remember our sick and pray for their healing, especially in mind and spirit. We lift up those who are struggling with moral dilemmas, and ask for your encouragement in their lives. We beseech you for those whose spirits are depressed, or unable to have faith, or unresponsive to the needs of others; let them be raised up above the clouds that engulf them and behold the glory of our inheritance. We offer our prayers for the president of our country, and for the Congress, and for members of the Supreme Court, that they may care for righteousness above expediency and justice above popularity. Grant wisdom and insight to the leaders of this congregation, and peace and companionship to all our visitors. Bless and keep our children and our children's children, and let your power be served by the offering we make of ourselves, our dreams, and our talents in this place, hallowed by the prayers and devotion of the saints, through Jesus Christ our Lord. Amen.

97

O God and Father of our Lord Jesus Christ, and Lord of the one true church, we tremble in awe before you when we realize what the church has often become in our time: a society of the satisfied, who no longer have a vision of the lostness of the world and the way of the cross; a fellowship of the crippled, who no longer have enough faith to be whole and strong in our spirits; a gathering of the critical, who carp and complain about things that could hardly be of less consequence; a body of the selfish, who want our name to be widely known and our rights to be carefully recognized; an encampment of the militant, who make war on one another over issues and doctrines that would never have concerned our Lord Jesus; and an outpost of the self-absorbed, who appear not even to realize that you have deserted us to our truant and insensitive ways, so that we stand alone in a world of evil and darkness, indistinguishable from the tortured shapes of other groups and organizations purporting to have some arcane reason for existence in the modern world. We erect great buildings, but ignore the poor and the homeless. We sing great hymns and anthems, but never listen to the songs of the world's lost children. We wear brilliant vestments, yet never notice the suffering of those who are clothed in rags. We glory in the great surgeons, corporate leaders, and media barons who belong to our congregations, yet rarely send them as missionaries to the enormous needs of Third World countries, or even into the poverty and crime of the ghettos in our own communities. We wrap ourselves in self-righteousness, setting ourselves up as judges of cultural trends and lifestyles, yet seldom embrace the people whose ways we are wont to deplore. How long, O God, will you suffer us to continue in our impossible vanity and conceit? When will your wrath descend on us like the fire of ten thousand suns, consuming us in flames of anger and holiness? Forgive us, dear God, for forgetting what church is all about: for forgetting Christ, who lived in self-imposed poverty and itinerancy in order to serve the gospel; for forgetting his crucifixion, which was to be our model of what happens to real faith; for forgetting our own smallness and truancy and inadequacy; for forgetting your love, not for the church, but for the world; not for the saved, but for the lost; not for the self-righteous, but for the humble and self-denigrating. Cleanse us of our arrogance and stupidity and self-importance, and return us to the all-consuming mission we once served as extensions of Christ in the world. Make us wise with heavenly wisdom, and gentle with heavenly love. Help us to rededicate ourselves to servant-hood, that we may care for the poorest, dirtiest, most diseased people on earth as if they were the dearest celebrities of our time. Imbue us with your Holy Spirit, that we may tear out these eyes that see as the world sees and, in our blindness, see as you see, so that your kingdom has a new chance to come on earth as it is in heaven, and the church may be redeemed along with the greatest of sinners, which indeed it has become. For we pray in the name of Christ, an act which in itself should fill us with awe and wonder and trembling. Amen.

98

O God, who has revealed yourself to us in history and in the Bible and in Christ and his disciples, we pray for revelation in our individual lives. Give us sensitivity to your divine presence in the people we meet and live with every day, and in the miracle of this universe, and in the existence of our own bodies and minds, and our own affections. It is a wonder, O God, that anything IS, that the world came into existence and that we are here to perceive it, to react to it, to care about it. Forgive us for living without sensitivity, for not noticing everything you have made, for being unaware of spiritual currents coursing around us every day that we live. Help us to find our way from darkness into light, that we may truly see and love the things you want us to see and love. Let your peace fill our hearts like the smell of roses and gardenias, and show us joy in the smallest routines of our day, from the taste of our breakfast toast to the feel of our pillows when we recline our heads on them at night. Bless the visitors in our midst, and let their being here today bring new love and clarity in their lives. Abide with any of our friends who are ill or who may be dealing with difficult problems of any kind. Anoint our children with your Spirit, that they may grow up with healthy minds and bodies. Make us generous to all who perform any service to us today, in our homes or in shops or restaurants, and give us altogether a sense of the glory of your creation, which we meet so bountifully on every hand, through Jesus Christ our Lord. Amen.

99

You are the Maker of everything, O God. We have made a few small things: homes and gardens and barbecue pits and a little money and our retirement plans. But you have made all that is: the mountains and oceans and waterfalls; the tall oaks and the tiny forget-me-nots; the great horses that work in the fields and the colorful hummingbirds that feed at our porches. You made our hearts to love and yearn and care for righteousness, and you have given us your Spirit that our hearts may find their way to you. We praise you, O God, for your tender mercies, and invoke your care on our world today. Send peace where there has been war, and relief where there has been distress. Watch over our friends and loved ones in other places. Bless all who visit among us today. Bestow serenity upon those whose hearts are troubled, and come to the aid of those who have need of anything. Teach us to hear you in the breeze that stirs the leaves and the voice of the child who cries, help us to see you in the faces of those we pass on the streets or the corridors of the mall, and let the love that was in Christ Jesus our Lord be in us as well, so that we learn to view everything in our lives in an entirely different light. For his name's sake. Amen.

100

In the deep silence, O God, we are reminded of our failure to follow Christ, to love one another, to forgive our enemies, and to seek your kingdom above all else in life. We confess to you the unworthiness of our thoughts and lives: all the impulses and desires that have been self-centered and self-serving, so that we have detracted from the good of the community and the life of the Spirit instead of building them up. Mend us, we pray, in all our flawed and broken places. Show us a higher way to be. Help us to love. We pray for all the lonely and hurting people we know; for all the elderly; for all who work in the service of others; for all who bear great responsibility; for those who teach our young; for the children themselves; for our visitors, and their lives and loved ones in other places; for those who occupy positions of authority and leadership in this church; and for all who attempt to lead in your church around the world. Let your Holy Spirit embrace our lives together, binding us in a sense of peace and security as brothers and sisters. And let us prove to be responsible heirs of the gospel of Christ and the ministry of love and reconciliation, now and in all the days to come. In the name of our dear Savior. Amen.

SEVEN

Communion Prayers

1

O God, in this world where many hunger and thirst, we are thankful for the humblest bread and the simplest drink. Yet this bread and drink are much more than that. They are the sacred reminder of your Son's death, and of the words of promise he spoke to his disciples, "Abide in me and I shall abide in you." Let the words come alive for us once more, and let the Presence live in our midst. Help us to see, to hear, to feel in these tokens the words of everlasting life and comfort, spoken to our restless hearts. We lift our thanksgiving for this table and its place in our lives. Forgive our sins and gather us together here as a family is gathered at the meal. Touch with rest and peace those who are troubled. Bind up the wounds of those who are hurting. Give love to those who feel estranged or bitter. Make us attentive to the world of needs around us. And let Christ be the head of the table and the head of our lives, this day and forever. Amen.

2

At this sacred table, O Lord, we shed our pretensions about ourselves. We know that we are sinners. We know we often fail in life—at work, at school, in our relationships, in our values, in our faith. But as you reached out to save Simon Peter and clutched him from the waves, reach out now to us and rescue us from all that threatens us. Teach us how to see your presence here. Give us thankful hearts for the mystery of this food and what it means to lives of faith. Send your Holy Spirit upon us to illumine the way we should think and believe when we have eaten and drunk. And bind us all together in the fellowship of your love from this moment on, forevermore. Amen.

3

God of harvest and God of board, God of hearth and God of love, we gather as your people to express our gratitude for the abundance of our life in the world. There is an abundance of *things* among us—homes, automobiles, food, computers, clothing, books, records, gadgets—and we are grateful for these. But more important, you have given us an abundance of spiritual and emotional wealth. You have surrounded us with loving family members, with a gracious community, with evidences of goodwill and encouragement. You have set us in a land where Christ has been freely preached, and the Word open for our reading. You have enticed us with moral examples. You have given us life around this table. For us, O God, the cup that overflows is the cup of salvation, the cup we lift today as we hear Jesus say, "Drink you all of it." Accept our thanksgiving for this cup, and for the bread of Christ's brokenness. Let us see and feel you here today. Make your presence real and tangible to us in the bread and cup. Anoint our hearts with love. Show us your face in one another, and bless your world through us as we turn to go from this place. Through him who was known to his disciples in the breaking of bread. Amen.

4

There is a special air at this table, O God, of tradition and memory, of depth and sacredness, of love and communion. We need such an air in our lives, that are prone to be lived with swiftness, thoughtlessness, and shallowness. It convicts us of sin and reminds us of our need for your forgiveness. Restore us, we pray, to fellowship with you and with one another, and to true integrity within ourselves. Let the health of this table overcome the disease of our hearts, minds, and bodies. May the presence of Jesus, that empowered the first disciples to become giants of the kingdom, enter our lives today, transforming them into lives of sanity, commitment, and generosity. May the bread and the cup become more than mere symbols on the table: may they become eternal food for our souls, whereby we grow into the gracious men and women you have designed us to be. Through Jesus Christ our Lord. Amen.

5
A Communion Prayer for Advent

Lord Jesus, whose coming we celebrate in this Advent season, we invoke your spirit now in this bread and cup of our salvation. Enable us to come in humility and repentance, being truly sorry for our lack of understanding and our failure of commitment, both to you and to your little ones in the world. Receive us in your grace and fill our hearts with great thanksgiving for every mercy we have received, including the fellowship around this table. And when we have eaten and drunk of your gifts, send us forth to our homes and workplaces with new excitement to be your witnesses, that your coming may be felt not in our lives only, but in the lives of all those we know and love. For your kingdom's sake. Amen.

6
A Communion Prayer for Christmas Eve

In the candlelight of Christmas Eve, O God, we gather around this sacred table to praise your name. On a cold, dark night in Bethlehem, you came among us as a little Child. Now, in the cool and darkness of this night, you are still with us. Your presence lingers in the very air we breathe. We tremble with a sense of your being. Our lives are full of sin and disobedience, and yet, in this place, we experience forgiveness and mercy. We are guilty of having gone our own ways without regard for you or your will for our lives, or the other people for whom we should have been concerned. But now, at this table, we feel that we are at home, that this is the center of the world toward which we have always journeyed. Receive us, dear God, in your loving-kindness. Pardon our sin, lift up our hearts, and renew a right spirit within us. Among all the gifts we shall give or receive this Christmas, let us count none dearer than this bread and this cup, the reminders of your sacrifice for us, the nourishment of eternal life. Of all the food we have eaten or shall ever eat, let none taste more wonderful than this. Of all the friends or family we have seen or intend to see, let none be more welcome than your Holy Spirit, whom we invite to come upon us now, making us one body in Christ, this Christmas Eve, and world without end. Hear us, O blessed Lord of Bethlehem, for the sake of your holy name. Amen.

7

Lord, we gather around this ageless table to remember your unchanging love and goodness to us. We celebrate your death, which was awful beyond description, and your triumphant Resurrection, which was glorious beyond telling, and your graceful presence here today, which, if we can only conceive it, is breathtaking. Accept our thanksgiving for the bread and the cup, and for the grace we take into our bodies even as we take your words into our minds and hearts. Let its power to heal our brokenness and unite us in love and generosity of spirit be manifest in our fellowship together. And let its gift of remembrance make us truly penitent before you, that life may begin afresh for us in this new year. For your name's sake. Amen.

8

O Lord, we thank you for this table, which is more important than any other table in the world, even the tables of
rulers where lands have been granted, and the tables of
generals where peace has been designed. For here, O Lord,
you gather your family in remembrance of a meal centuries
ago and visit your people as you did then. We are grateful
for daily bread, for the food of our tables—for biscuits and
hams and chickens and beans and potatoes and rice—but
more grateful for this bread, which in our hearts is your
own body broken for us on the cross. We praise you for
drink—for water and milk and tea and coffee and ale and
soft drinks and all the precious liquids that sustain our
bodies—but praise you more for this juice of the vine,
which in our hearts is your blood, shed for our sin at
Calvary. Come now, Lord Jesus, and be present at this table
as we eat and drink. Enter every lowly and repentant heart
to renew our lives and love and fellowship. Let your Holy
Spirit cleanse us of all the hate and resentment and brokenness of spirit that now clutter our existence, and make
us new men and women and boys and girls, eager to go
into the world where we live and reclaim it for you as part
of your eternal kingdom. For you have bought us at the
price of your own life, and thus won our allegiance forever.
Amen.

9

This is your table, Lord, not ours. We have no right of place
here. None of us deserves to sit at your right hand. We are
all sinners saved by grace. We have all betrayed your love.
We have hated, envied, lusted, competed, stolen, denied,
broken, and in some ways even killed. Yet you have given
your body to be mutilated for us, you have had your veins
broken and emptied of blood for us. What a feast of love
you have given us! What priceless redemption you have
bestowed upon us. Forgive us once more, dear Christ, and

receive us as repentant followers who cannot live without this table. Lift us from our brokenness and despondency as you lifted your first disciples, and make us into a church of power in the kingdom. Baptize us in your Holy Spirit, that all things may become new and that this table may truly sit at the center of our lives. For yours are the kingdom and the power and the glory forever. Amen.

10

Love sets a table here, Lord, we know that. There is nowhere else in all the world where we feel it as surely as we feel it here. The Lord of the universe says, "This is my body, broken for you. This is my blood, shed for the remission of your sins." We taste the bread, we drink the cup, we feel new life, *your* life, filling our own. The dark places of our souls are brought to light. The emptiness and the failures are dismissed. We eat and drink forgiveness. We are brought together in love and fellowship. Our sensibilities are renewed. Our hope is reborn. It is your table, Lord, and it is a table of love. Help us to eat and drink worthily, by acknowledging our unworthiness. And let the tokens of bread and juice be a feast to our souls, renewing, restoring, rebuilding, rekindling, remaking us in your image, in the image of love. You know we are thankful. You know we love you. You know everything. You *know* we love you. Amen.

11

Before this blessed table, O God, we come as humble beggars. The person in finest cloth is uncovered before your eyes, and the one of noblest mind is no more than a little child. The only glory any of us enjoys here is the glory of your Son who died on Calvary and commanded us to eat this bread and drink this cup in his memory. We thank you for his life and teachings, and for the ministry of his death and resurrection—for his risen presence here among us now. Open our eyes to that presence through the work of your Holy Spirit, and let us pledge ourselves once more to your kingdom and to the service of your little ones throughout the world, for we ask it in your holy name. Amen.

12

When we survey this wondrous table, O God, our hearts are almost too full for words. To think that you have given your only Son to suffer and die on the cross in our behalf, and then have spread this table before us, filled with bread and wine as a reminder of your covenant of grace, is quite overwhelming. Behold the gratitude we feel in the promises of faithfulness we are making now, each in our silent meeting with you, and in the newness of life by which we live when we leave this place. Let your Holy Spirit come upon us, assuring us of forgiveness, lifting our eyes to new challenges for ourselves and this church, and binding us together in love and fellowship. For your name's sake. Amen.

EIGHT

Benedictions

1

May the God who existed before the creation itself come presently into your hearts and lives and abide there always, that you may be forever young in your spirits and enjoy life everlasting, through Jesus Christ our Lord. Amen.

2

Now may God, who calls to us from every singing bird and flowering bush, but more poignantly from a cross and empty tomb, send you forth as sons and daughters of the Resurrection to be joyous and radiant people, transformed and transforming forevermore. In the name of the Father, Son, and Holy Spirit. Amen.

3

Now may God, who has given us the good news of the divine rule in Christ Jesus, give us also with him the passion and desire to serve that rule, now and forever, in the name of the Father, Son, and Holy Spirit. Amen.

4

Now may God, who has fed us at this table with the gift of the divine Son, continue to feed us through this week on the Holy Spirit, that we may be led into every pathway intended for us and possess the joy that has been promised us, through Jesus Christ our Lord. Amen.

5

Now may God, who created the world and all that is in it, teach us to live faithfully as stewards of everything around us, and to love one another with an unceasing love, through Jesus Christ our Lord. Amen.

6

May the God of life and truth be real to you this week in all the affairs of your life, both great and small, and may the purpose of the divine will fill your hearts with joy and excitement now and forever, through Jesus Christ our Lord. Amen.

7

May the risen Lord meet us today wherever we go; may he dispel the clouds and make the sun shine in our souls; may he use us to touch the lives of others, blessing the poor in spirit and alleviating the ills of the world; and may his name be praised now and forever, time without end. Amen.

8

Now may God, who calls us on our way and stands waiting for us at the end of the journey, be with us at every step, in the name of the Father, Son, and Holy Spirit. Amen.

9

Now may God, who has given us every opportunity to remember the divine grace in Jesus Christ, make us mindful of the holy presence this day and forevermore, that we may do justice, love mercy, and walk humbly in the name of the Father, Son, and Holy Spirit. Amen.

10

Now may God, who has caused us to hear a good word and respond to it with our hearts, establish our way into the lives of those who have not yet heard, that they too may be included in our community, and we may praise and glorify God together, now and forevermore. Amen.

11

Now may God, who dwells in mystery and holiness, preserve you and yours this day and in all days to come, guiding and sustaining you in times of trial, and bringing you at last to the heavenly rest, in the name of the Father, Son, and Holy Spirit. Amen.

12

Now may God, who has loved us with a love beyond all telling, send us forth to care for the world around us and to share the good news of that love, in the name of the Father, Son, and Holy Spirit. Amen.

13

Now may God, whose peace passes all human understanding, keep your minds and hearts in eternal blessedness today and evermore. Amen.

14

Now may God, who spoke to us in the life and death and Resurrection of Jesus Christ, hear us as we respond this week through our loving and faithful actions for all Christ's little ones. In the name of the Father, Son, and Holy Spirit. Amen.

15

We have sung, and the song continues to sing in our hearts. We have prayed, and the sense of presence now follows us as an aura. We have heard the Word, and it has shown us how to live. Now let us go from here to sing and pray and witness, and may God prepare our way in the wilderness, in the name of the Father, Son, and Holy Spirit. Amen.

16

Now may God, who has sat at table with us, continue with us wherever we go, and sit at table with us always. Through Jesus Christ our Lord. Amen.

17

May all the roads you travel be upward roads, rising to meet Christ, and may you travel them as easily as if they were downward roads, kept in the love of him who inhabits all roads, watching over his favorite travelers. In the name of the Father, Son, and Holy Spirit. Amen.

18

Now may God, who has brought again from the dead our Lord Jesus Christ, the great shepherd of the sheep, give us such a sense of the life to come that we have no hesitance to live in his kingdom this week, but surrender all that we are and have to his blessed name, now and forever. Amen.

19

Now may God, who has always been full of surprises, surprise you this week by reminding you of grace in at least four places where you never thought to look for it. In the name of the Creator, Child, and Holy Spirit. Amen.

20

Now may God, who has loved us and given us the Savior to die for our sins, give us life in his name and love for all created things, in the name of the Father, Son, and Holy Spirit. Amen.

21

Now may God, who created us a special people in Christ Jesus, lead us into the fullness of life for which we were intended, and give us peace and love to share with others wherever we go, in the name of the Father, Son, and Holy Spirit. Amen.

22

Now may God, who has sent Jesus into the world to save us from sin and reconcile us to holiness, give us the desire and the strength to follow Christ today and throughout this week, in the name of the Father, Son, and Holy Spirit. Amen.

23

Now may God, who has given us Jesus Christ to be our Lord and Savior, continue to shed the divine grace upon us, leading us into eternal love and service today and in all the days to come. In the name of the Father, Son, and Holy Spirit. Amen.

24

Now may God, who sent Christ into the world to die for our sins, implant in your hearts a song that will never die, and may the music of your faith make the whole world turn upon a divine rhythm. In the name of the Father, Son, and Holy Spirit. Amen.

25

Now may God, who has many things to show us, give us receptive hearts and spirits, and keep us all in tender, loving care until we meet again. In the name of the Father, Son, and Holy Spirit. Amen.

26

Now may God, who gives us life and love, nourish us with the sunlight of the divine presence, that we may grow in all spiritual graces. In the name of the Father, Son, and Holy Spirit. Amen.

27

Now may God, who is able to stay our lives when all around us goes awry and bring us to eternal salvation in perfect grace, bless you and keep you in the divine will, which is perfect peace, through Jesus Christ our Lord. Amen.

28

Now may the grace of God bring joy and peace to your hearts, and give you strength for your journeys, this day and evermore. In the name of the Father, Son, and Holy Spirit. Amen.

29

Now may God, who has given us so many blessings that we cannot count them, give us also thankful hearts, that we may find true blessedness, in the name of the Father, Son, and Holy Spirit. Amen.

30

A Benediction for Advent

Now may God, who was celebrated by angels' songs and worshiped by shepherds from the hillsides, anoint us with the true spirit of Christmas, that we too may sing and worship, now and forever, in the name of the Father, Son, and Holy Spirit. Amen.

31

A Benediction for Christmas Eve

May God, who gave us the Christ Child in the stable of Bethlehem, continue to show us mercy in the love and graciousness of Christmas, and may the Christ Child whose glory filled the sky dwell in each of us tonight. In the name of the Father, and the Son, and the Holy Spirit. Amen.

32
A Benediction for Holy Week

And now may God, who sustained our Lord Jesus in the hour of his trial, undergird you with faith and hope and love for your own trials, in this hour and throughout this holy week, in the name of the Father, Son, and Holy Ghost. Amen.

33

Now may the Spirit that has brought us here return us on our way with joy and favor, and may this day be one of the best you've ever had, in the name of the Father, Son, and Holy Spirit. Amen.

34

Now may God, who gives us the energy to lead productive and fruitful lives, teach us also to seek quiet and solitary places, where we may be filled with the divine presence and renewed for meaningful living, in the name of the Father, Son, and Holy Spirit. Amen.

35
A Benediction for a Maundy Thursday Service

May God be with us through this night; may we watch prayerfully through the day tomorrow, remembering our Lord's death; may love overcome any sense of estrangement within us; and may our spirits rise with Christ on Easter morn, full of victory and hope. Amen.

36
A Benediction for Easter Sunday

Now may God, who has raised Jesus Christ from the dead and made him "Victor o'er the dark domain," raise us all from our apathy and indecision, and make us true disciples this week and forever more. In the name of the Father, Son, and Holy Spirit. Amen.

37

Now may God, who does indeed make it possible for us to walk with Christ, continue to bless us with his loving presence, and keep us together in spirit even when we are absent from one another, in the name of the Father, Son, and Holy Spirit. Amen.

38

Now may God, who has ordained the seasons of the year, and the seasons of life as well, grant you serenity and joy in this season of your soul, and in the world to come everlasting life, through Jesus who died and lives forevermore. Amen.

39

Now may God, the Almighty One who lives in holiness and mystery beyond our human understanding, continue to give us peace and mercy, and to lead us to love one another, in the name of the Father, Son, and Holy Spirit. Amen.

40

Now let us go from this place in a spirit of love and forgiveness, with our hearts mended and our souls encouraged, and may God bless you forever, in the name of the Father, Son, and Holy Spirit. Amen.

41

May the God of our Lord Jesus Christ, who gives us the power to discern truth from falsehood and authenticity from inauthenticity, give us also the love to be at peace with all persons of goodwill, that we may forever serve truth and justice in the world and come at last to our heavenly rest with full hearts and a sense of joy. In the name of the Father, Son, and Holy Spirit. Amen.

42

Now may the God who has given us life so abundantly give us also a spirit to enjoy and celebrate it, and to live singing and dancing in the holy presence. In the name of the Father, Son, and Holy Spirit. Amen.

43

Now may the grace of God, made known to us in the love and fellowship we have enjoyed so abundantly here today, be and abide with us all, this day and forever. In the name of the Father, Son, and Holy Ghost. Amen.

44

Now may God, who has made all things bright and beautiful, make your way to be bright and beautiful, and give you peace now and forever, in the name of the Father, Son, and Holy Spirit. Amen.

45

Now may God, who has smiled on us with divine favor, teach us to smile on the world with a similar favor, and be joyous in our faith, in the name of the Father, Son, and Holy Spirit. Amen.

46

Let us go from this place strengthened and blessed by the eternal presence we have felt here, and be glad and loving to all we meet, for we have been with the Lord, in the name of the Father, Son, and Holy Spirit. Amen.

47

Now may God, who has given us the possibility of worlds yet undiscovered, give us the grace and courage to explore and enjoy them, in the name of the Father, Son, and Holy Spirit. Amen.

48

Go back now to your world of computers and shopping malls and superhighways; but remember that it is not as real as the world you are leaving here, where we have communed with God and spoken of love and death and eternal life; in the name of the Father, Child, and Holy Spirit. Amen.

49

May God smile upon you this day with eternal love and favor, and may you know it, so that you are encouraged to love your life and to celebrate it, even when there may be pain and difficulty, in the name of the Father, the Son, and the Holy Spirit. Amen.

50

Now may the peace of God, that is abundantly more than we could ever hope or dream, be upon and abide within the reader of this book, and upon all who offer these prayers and all who hear them, now and forever, through Jesus Christ our Lord. Amen.